# Kitesurfing

## The Complete Guide

### 2nd Edition

*Ian Currer*

## Kitesurfing The Complete Guide  (Edition 2) 2007

Published by: Northern Paragliding Ltd
Dalefoot, Mallerstang, Kirkby Stephen, Cumbria CA17 4JT, UK
www.northern-paragliding.com

First edition published by Lakes Paragliding 2002 ISBN: 0-9542896-0-9

Second revised and updated edition published by Northern Paragliding Ltd June 2007.

British Library Cataloguing in Publishing Data

A catalogue record for this book is available from the British Library.

ISBN: (ISBN-10): 0-9542896-1-7    (ISBN-13): 978-0-9542896-1-4

Text: Ian Currer

Technical Editor: Andy Gratwick (on behalf of the British Kitesurfing Association)

Illustrations: David Barber & Neil Cruickshank

Page layout & design: Neil Cruickshank

Printed and bound: Perfils Spain.

# Contents

# Acknowledgements

**I would like to thank the following people and companies for their support in producing both this edition and the original edition of this book.**

Neil Cruickshank for all the layout and organisation

Dave Barber for the illustrations

Andy Gratwick (BKSA training officer) for the technical editing

Jacky Bevan for the proof reading

Richard Robinson of Cordee book distribution

Sportif and Club Mistral in Egypt

Andre Carder, instructor at Club Mistral for his instruction and editorial input.

Paul Jobin (The founding chairman of the BKSA) and TKC sales

Richard Gowers and the BKSA team

Gus of www.extremesportphotos.com for the shots

Mike Birt of Surfstore

Airush

Cabrinha

Flexifoil

And all the readers and riders who have supported the project, contributed advice, feedback and pictures.

Ian Currer, June 2007

# Foreword

Since starting in watersports 28 years ago something new has always grabbed my attention every few years – today it is Kitesurfing

Discovering how to fly off a wave some 20 years ago windsurfing, the need to get air has always been a passion for me.

From the first pictures of kitesurfing I saw with Laird Hamilton in the mid 90's I was eager to give it ago, it wasn't until 1999 I took to the water when equipment became  generally available.

To say it was hard to learn was an understatement!  – with no one to ask for advice or teach you.  The kit was awful with little or no safety devices – however I was determined.

The first year saw a lot of walking back up the beach,  but eventually with the progression in equipment I managed to go upwind and started to jump – this was kitesurfing!

Since then I haven't looked back – You can ride so many boards, Twintip, surfboard, wakeskate, wakeboard, mutant, skimboard – all with the same kite and in so many waterstates – glassy flat offshore to pumping 30 ft waves. Jumping is amazing!

Glad to say it is now so much easier and safer than it was back in '99.

Learners can now be up and riding in 2-3 days after doing a course. However there is still a vast amount of information that you require to be a safe and competent kitesurfer.

This book by Ian Currer answers all of these questions and more in this invaluable guide to anyone,- be they new to kitesurfing or a seasoned veteran  (I certainly learnt a thing or two).

The book is set out clearly and precisely with excellent photo's and illustrations, and takes you step by step through all the information you should require.

Welcome to the world of Kitesurfing – I look forward to  welcoming you to our association and seeing you on the water – beware though it is addictive!

Ride Safe

Richard Gowers

Chairman: British Kite Surfing Association

info@kitesurfing.org

www.kitesurfing.org

# Introduction

Congratulations! If you have started, or are thinking of starting kitesurfing, your dreams of skimming the water and performing spectacular jumps will soon be real.

This new and spectacular sport combines the speed and thrills of windsurfing with the radical tricks of wakeboarding and offers the unique potential for huge jumps even from flat water. The kit is comparatively small, there is no need for a boat, and it can be done in winds varying from just 8 or 10 knots right up to howling conditions.

Kitesurfing is easy to learn. It is perfectly possible to get blasting in just a few days, or even just a few hours if you have some related experience such as power kite flying, windsurfing or wakeboarding.

There will be many challenges of course, and it will take some time and effort and quite a few wipeouts before you become a competent kitesurfer, but it will be worth it for the rare experience of being one of the few to master the newest and most exhilarating of sports.

This handbook is meant as an aid to learning, to be referred to before, during and after your training. It is not meant as a do-it-yourself manual. Kites are usually thought of as toys, but large traction kites are by nature very powerful and deserve considerable respect. Kitesurfing could result in injury or even death, particularly if attempted in the wrong place or the wrong weather conditions.

The only safe way to learn is to be trained by a competent, qualified instructor. In the UK we very strongly recommend a BKSA recognised school.

BKSA instructors are independently assessed by the association. If training elsewhere you may not have access to BKSA instructors. In this case you should check that your trainer is properly qualified.

Occasionally in this book kitesurfers are referred to as 'he' - this is simply for the sake of writing style. Kitesurfing is of course a sport that can be equally well enjoyed by both men and women.

Enjoy!

# A Brief History

Modern kite surfing may seem to have a shorter history than most sports, but its roots go back quite a way. For several thousand years the Chinese, in particular, have been flying kites. Legend has it that the first kite was invented by a Chinese farmer, who tied a string to his hat to prevent him from losing it when it was blown off in the wind.

There is little doubt that man-lifting kites have been used for a very long time. Marco Polo remarked that only a fool or a drunkard would allow himself to be lifted into the air by a kite, and this was in the thirteenth century! The power of a good-sized kite on a breezy day was clearly well understood. Perhaps these kites were used to power small watercraft - we do not know - but it is certain that the concept of body-dragging is not a new invention!

Like many sports, kitesurfing evolved from a fusion of existing skills and equipment; water-skiing & wakeboarding, windsurfing, snowboarding and paragliding have all played their part, and of course kites themselves, as mentioned, have been around a very long time.

Benjamin Franklin, best known for his experiments in 1752 with kites and lightning, was also a great innovator and lover of kites as a youth, and he often tied a large kite to his boat to get a free ride.

In 1825 George Pocock, an English schoolteacher, and some of his friends, travelled regularly in a carriage pulled

A 17th Century British kite flyer!

Getting ready for some serious powerkite flying; these 10ft span kites are being stacked to form a 'Jacobs ladder' - a technique used in the earliest attempts at kitesurfing

by a stack of kites - on one occasion achieving a speed of 30 miles an hour.

The very first instances of kitesurfing we know of were stories of pioneers who managed to power themselves, usually on water skis, using a stack of conventional kites - the 'Jacobs ladder' approach, still popular with power kite flyers today.

At the end of the sixties another development, the ram-air parachute, was transforming the skydiving world, with new rigs that actually flew like wings rather than just slowing the fall. In the early eighties, this technology was taken another step with the use of high-performance airfoils and new materials, and foot launched paragliders capable of soaring flight appeared.

The manufacturers of these wings made many refinements to the flexible airfoil and a good proportion are active today in

Twin-tip kitesurf boards show many similarities to wakeboards

producing high-performance kites for kitesurfing.

Ram-air foils were soon popular for recreational kites too, and unlike previous kite design that relied simply on drag, the new shapes used airfoil sections and generated lift as well, offering twice the power for the same area. Powerkiting was born, and spin-offs like buggies and mountain (ATB) boards were quick to follow. Some kitesurfing was taking place already, as water was an obvious place to use the power of these wings. In 1988, Cory Roesler won the Johnnie Walker speed sailing championships for craft with a 10m sail or less. By using water-skis and a kite, he beat the next nearest competitor by a huge margin, demonstrating the inherent superiority of a moving kite to a static sail.

Of course there was already a group of sailors who had simple equipment and

A modern paraglider

high speed as their main interests. It was not long before the windsurfing fraternity entered the picture...

Windsurfing is a highly popular sport that has been in existence for many years. Driven by both manufacturers and sailors, the sport has become increasingly technical, with performance advances diminishing each year.

Like some other sports, the gulf between the experts and the beginners was growing ever larger. It is only comparatively recently that the focus has once again switched to making the sport user-friendly for a wider range of people.

Windsurfing is still not an easy sport to learn!

Although replacing the sail of a windsurfer with a kite seems fairly obvious, there are a number of practical problems. With no mast foot pressure the dynamics of the whole system are changed quite radically. The rider's weight must be moved forward towards the middle of the board, and even if the

foot straps are moved to allow this, a windsurf board is often too large to sail easily with a kite.

However the appeal of a 'new' wind-powered watersport to windsurfers is easy to see, particularly one that allows such a great potential for jumps and performance in lighter winds, and many of the skills are transferable.

What was needed was an application of the skills of windsurfers and kiting, together with the effort to overcome the technical problems of making kitesurfing a practical proposition. Fortunately for us, the Legaignoux brothers, Dominique and Bruno, based in northwest France, had the combination of skills and vision to overcome the difficulties and design the original Wipika (Wind Powered Inflatable Kite Aircraft).

In fact, the original idea was to use a marine kite to power a catamaran or a conventional vessel should its engine fail, either to tow it, or simply to keep it headed into the waves in a storm. They patented their idea in 1985, and although

Many of the earliest pioneers came from a windsurfing background.

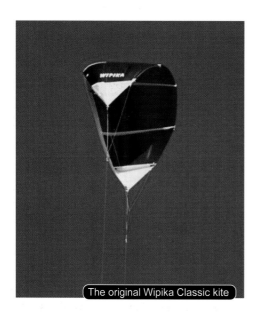

The original Wipika Classic kite

Manu Bertin with an early Wipika kite, circa 1995

the brothers may have considered using their kites for recreation, it was not until a fellow Frenchman and professional windsurfer Emmanuel Bertin started using the Wipika kite with a modified surfboard that the real potential of making upwind progress was feasible, and a whole new sport was realized.

Manu had already been interested in using a kite to power a board, and had spent some time in Hawaii with Laird Hamiliton (a name familiar to all surfers) trying to perfect the art of kite-powered surfing. With the advent of the Wipika inflatable kites, this really started to come together, and Bertin (whose nickname Manu means 'bird' in the Hawaiian language) was soon making real progress and started teaching others. One of his early pupils was Robbie Naish whose company Naish sails was, and still is, a major player in the windsurfing, and later the kitesurfing industry.

There were a few problems to overcome. The first hurdle, that of finding a suitable board, was solved quite easily, simply by modifying existing surfboards or wakeboards with foot straps screwed into the appropriate positions. Manu asked an Italian shaper, Roberto Ricci, who came up with the first dedicated board. It included elements of a surf-board (outline), a windsurfing wave board ( radical nose rocker) and a snowboard (sharp rails).

Another problem was simply controlling such a powerful kite without too much strain on the arms. The bar system with a loop that could be 'hooked into' with a harness, was a useful piece of windsurfing-derived technology that made prolonged use possible.

The greatest challenge, however, was re-launching the kite from the water. Both rigid 'hang-glider' types and ram-air kites have an unfortunate habit of remaining down once wet, either because part of the structure becomes submerged or because water gets inside the cells.

Perhaps the single most important development that made kitesurfing practical was the design of the Legaignoux inflatable kite. It was the combination of a single-skinned design supported by inflatable spars and the 'arc' shape which worked so well. The inflated kite is of course very buoyant, which made it impossible to submerge. The curved shape prevented the kite from lying flat on the surface, so given sufficient wind, the downed kite would easily drift to full line stretch position and could be re-launched without the problems of water becoming trapped inside any structure or cells.

The lifting performance of this type of kite is relatively poor, but that is easily remedied simply by using a greater surface area, and the re-launchability made it the easiest by far for the new kitesurfer to use. Finally, having produced a kite that will self launch, there is the problem of how to stop it dragging you forever if you should lose control! The introduction of leashes and quick release mechanisms took care of this final barrier.

All the elements were in place to enable kitesurfing to become a practical sport.

Wipika began producing kites for the new sport, and not long afterwards Robby Naish made an agreement with the Legaignoux brothers and began production of his own kite range.

Nice! *(Photo: Tracey Kraft, Cabrinha)*

These earliest pioneers have been joined by many more companies and a range of different designs. Most companies are using a variation on the inflatable spar design; many are licensed users of the Legaignoux patent and many more designers are working on producing innovative solutions to the challenges of the sport.

Over the last few years, as the sport has grown, there has been an explosion of development in the equipment, the techniques and the standard of tuition available.

Twin-tip and asymmetric boards, ram-air and high aspect ratio, bow, and hybrid kites and professional schools have all come into being. National and international associations have grown rapidly, and while it is still early days for the sport, the future is looking good.

The sport first became popular in places such as the south of France and other Mediterranean beaches, Florida, Hawaii and other similar places. Today kitesurfers are to be found from Scandinavia to Egypt - in fact just about anywhere in the world with favourable winds and suitable beaches.

Windsurfers, wakeboarders, powerkiters and paraglider pilots have all been attracted into this new sport. Its popularity is still growing, and it is surely inevitable that its unique appeal will continue to spread and it will become as familiar a sight as dinghies and windsurfers on lakes and beaches throughout the world.

# Getting Started

Kitesurfing is a great sport, but to ride safely and make good progress you will need training. Kitesurfing can be extremely dangerous, both to the participant and others, if practiced incorrectly or in unsuitable conditions.

Lessons from a BKSA (or other national body) instructor are very strongly recommended. This book is laid out in pretty much the order that the subjects and techniques will come up. You may need to jump around and refer back to some chapters, but it is logical to start out with an overview of the likely training programme.

Before you even start kitesurfing, you can help yourself a lot by becoming familiar with power kites in general. Students who have spent a few hours practicing with a traction kite are always better prepared and progress faster than those who start from scratch.

Kitesurfing can be fairly demanding to learn, so the best way is to break it down into manageable chunks and work at each skill before progressing to the next. It is essential to get those critical early lessons from an instructor at an approved school. It is very tempting to just buy all the gear and take yourself off to the nearest beach, but this method has a high failure rate and is very dangerous.

## The Training System

In the UK the BKSA look after the training and qualifying of students, instructors and schools. They set a high standard in terms of safety and quality and are internationally recognised for their professionalism.

Different countries and different training operations will use slightly varying techniques and systems. This outline is intended as a general guide as to what you should expect. (If it is radically different it is worth asking why!)

A good course will always begin with students being warned of the dangers involved in a sport like kitesurfing; a check should be made of their fitness and ability to swim. Students should sign up for membership of their national association to ensure that they are riding with proper insurance cover. For obvious reasons, a contact address and details need

Rule Number 1: Get good instruction

to be taken by the instructor before training commences. The school should provide helmets and buoyancy aids for pupils.

### 1. Site Assessment: Choosing a good site & correct wind conditions

The site must be large enough to allow at least 4 line lengths downwind of the flying area without any obstruction. The ideal is to have a large area of shallow water with a smooth bottom; in this case it is not a problem if you are pulled over and dragged, but of course not every training centre has this luxury, and it is perfectly reasonable to do the initial phases of your training on dry land. Sandy beaches are ideal, but grass or some other smooth surface that will not damage the kite can also be used.

There must be no swimming areas, launch zones for windsurfers or boats or other hazards like rocks, reefs or jetties immediately downwind, as it is always possible for a gust to drag you that way. On land, the same applies to power lines, nearby airports or other dangerous hazards, and the area should be well away from roads, so that an escaped kite will

An ideal launch area *(Photo: Advance)*

not cause anyone else a problem. It is critical that consideration is given to other people; an out-of-control kite can seriously injure a swimmer or a passer-by, and it may be necessary to walk a long way to find an unpopulated bit of lagoon, beach or field. If others do come near you, the kite must always be either hoisted to the zenith position and controlled, or landed and secured before they get within range!

The wind should be a reasonable breeze, enough to allow you to feel the power when the kite is moving fast. If you cannot stand still with the kite in the safe position above you, the wind is too strong or the kite chosen is too big.

If the wind is light, or you are training in the water, a full size traction kite may be used, but if it is a good wind, especially if you are doing this phase of your training on the beach or in a field, starting with a smaller training kite, perhaps of 2 or 3 square metres, is recommended.

If training in the water, it is important that a drift downwind cannot take you into deep water, so on coastal sites the wind must be primarily cross-shore.

Correct wind-speed and direction are critical to safety and progress.

## 2. An introduction to power kites.

The first job is to check the gear and learn how to set it up. This may include disentangling lines and pumping up inflatable kites and securing them with sand, connecting the lines with lark's head knots, and the control bar and safety leash. Once the gear is ready, the instructor will demonstrate how to launch the kite and control it using the bar. Once demonstrated, each student will have a turn at practising the launch and control technique.

## 3. The window and safe (zenith) position

This will be explained and demonstrated.

## 4. Control exercises

These will typically be to fly the kite to the edges of the window . During this exercise the kite should be controlled slowly and smoothly, and the correct stance with feet together, knees flexed and straight arms should be mastered.

## 5. Working the kite and controlling power

These exercises are to introduce the control patterns you will need on the water, doing vertical 'S' patterns on one side of the window only, then moving on to horizontal 'S' patterns through the central power band.

As you work the kite, there may be enough force to drag you through the water or down the beach or field (this is why sand is the best solid surface). A smooth pattern with constant power should result in a good straight consistent drag downwind. Smooth straight pulls at this stage will translate into long smooth rides on the board later, so it is

The wind is unpredictable; ideally you need a school with a good range of equipment to make the most of light or strong conditions. This is Club Mistral, Safaga, Egypt.

worth practising now.

### 6. The emergency drop

Inevitably at some point you will need to stop the kite, due to other water users or some other hazard, or just because you need to sort yourself out. Any reasonable kite will be fitted with a leash that enables you to simply drop the bar and remain in contact with the kite as it flutters down.

### 7. Using the harness

This exercise covers setting up and hooking into the harness and controlling the kite through the bar with one hand.

### 8. The start

The final exercise is to practise the start. Begin by sitting in shallow water.

Fly the kite to high in the' back' half of the window, then turn it hard and dive it through the power band in the leading half of the window. This will generate a surge of power and start you moving. Reverse the bar to stop it diving into the ground and go straight into a smooth 'S' pattern in the front half of the window. This will keep you powered up and moving at an angle.

### 9. Body-dragging exercises

There are three body-dragging exercises you will need to master:

Working the kite for power.

Working on one side of the window for directional control.

Body-dragging cross-wind (using one hand as a rudder).

### 10. Theory

You will be trained about the sectors of the window, how to increase and decrease power and where to place the kite for best effect in different situations (e.g. higher up for more down-wind beats), basic weather and site assessment.

### 11. Re-launching the kite from the water techniques

First standing, and then from a prone or supine position. This is far easier in shallow water, when you can stand on the bottom and prevent drifting.

### 12. Introducing the board

A look-out and safety boat are a huge advantage when learning.

Learning how to handle the board in the water, and how to get your feet into the board straps correctly while controlling the kite with one hand.

## 13. Starting on the board

This will take quite a bit of practice, as you will now be trying to work the kite smoothly, maintain balance and the correct stance and foot steer the board, at the same time as keeping a lookout ahead.

Starting with the board; a helmet and bouyancy aid are essential safety items.

It is very useful to practice the start technique on the beach with the help of a friend or instructor.

## 14. Controlling power, speed and direction

Speed management and learning to edge the board to make progress upwind. Almost all modern kites will feature a de-power system, which allows you to change the angle of attack of the kite and so reduce (or increase) the available force and alter the speed of the kite. Some time will be spent learning to manage your particular kit to the best advantage.

## 15. Self rescue and dealing with problems

You need to learn about how to pack your kite in the water and self-rescue techniques.

## 16. Turning

You will learn how to switch direction; using a twin tip board this is straightforward; if using a directional, you will need to master 'gybing' techniques.

### 17. Different kite types.

More advanced exercises include jumping, wave riding, achieving speed, and then possibly different equipment such as wake boards with bindings, etc. These are generally not included in a training syllabus, but become more applicable with experience.

### 18 Packing & care of your kit

See Chapter 21 for more info.

The BKSA have a large network of quality checked schools and instructors; many are listed in the information section of this book, and up-to-date information and links to schools can be found on their website at www.kitesurfing.org.

Learning at a good school gives you access to an enormous array of the latest equipment.

# Health and Safety

Kites and kitesurfing exist for just one purpose - because they are fun; essentially they are just big toys.

However, the power of these playthings is sufficient to cause injury or worse if they are misused and anyone wishing to use one must bear in mind a few simple safety considerations.

## Health Considerations

Are you healthy enough to participate? If you are feeling unwell or are nursing a previous injury or have some problem that would prevent you from coping with being pulled over or being dragged; then it is probably wise to give this a miss.

All training centres will provide a buoyancy aid, but it is still almost inevitable that you will be submerged a few times and you will get water up your nose, in your sinuses and down your throat at some point.

Once in the water you may quickly find

yourself facing a long swim, and in wavy conditions you will certainly get a good ducking. Obviously being a strong swimmer and at home in the water is a definite prerequisite for a kitesurfer.

Medical conditions such as heart problems or diabetes may also be a hazard, as your body will be subjected to a great deal of strain and your energy demands when hammering through rough water at 20 knots are extremely high! Perhaps the most problematical aspect for many people is the fact that unlike some sports, you cannot necessarily simply stop when you have had enough. Even if you are cold, tired and waterlogged you may still need to be able to summon the effort to sail, paddle or wade back to your start point.

## General Safety

Kitesurfing can be easy; it can certainly look very easy, but do be realistic when deciding what you are capable of. It is better to be on the beach wishing you were out there, than out there wishing you were on the beach!

In practical terms you do need to be able to assess the weather situation, and whether your equipment is appropriate. This means the wind strength, the direction, the gustiness, and the state of the water. Like all water sports it is important that the kitesurfer is aware not only of the wave height and direction, but also the state of the tide and currents if sailing on the sea. Water temperature and the wind chill are also factors that will determine how much time you can safely spend out riding.

Not every ride is a smooth one!

There are three elements to kitesurfing safely: the conditions, the kit being used and the human factors of confidence and decision-making. The three are closely related and most accidents occur when two or more elements combine to go wrong!

Choosing suitable conditions is critical, and you should always try to be realistic about how you would cope if, for example, a gust of wind picked you up at your chosen launch spot. If there is no margin for error you are asking for trouble. The second area is that of your kit. Is it the right size and level and is it well maintained? Most importantly, do your safety systems work properly?

There are further chapters in this book to help you make this kind of evaluation.

Human factors of judgment and confidence are more important than swimming ability! If you are frightened or fearful about launching your kite then do not do it.

As all instructors know, extreme stress makes it very hard to learn and increases your risk of accident or injury. This is a sport after all, and it is meant to be fun!

Overconfidence is a term that crops up frequently in accident reports for all adventure sports.

Kitesurfing requires a good level of confidence and self-belief, but it must be tempered with a realistic view of your own abilities!

If you have driven a hundred miles to get to this spot, and your girlfriend/ boyfriend/ mother/ family or TV crew are

Push your limits - but push them carefully!

Board Rider: Tom Hebert Photographer: John Carter

all waiting for you to go, but conditions are dodgy, the smart rider will say 'It's too much for me and I am going to wait for it to improve.' (Try practicing this in the mirror!)

Look at the big picture! Breaking a line, ditching a kite and being unable to re-launch it in the sea with an offshore wind, or with an ebbing tide is a lot more serious than the same situation on a lake or with a cross-shore breeze. Therefore it is clear that you need to be more cautious about sailing alone, or strong conditions in certain circumstances. Trying new things and especially stronger weather conditions is best done when there is safety boat cover on hand.

The best recommendation is to always try and ride with other kitesurfers and take advice from those with the best local knowledge and experience. Never sail in poor visibility, whether caused by poor weather or by the onset of dusk; the risks of disorientation and collision are obviously magnified.

If you do choose to sail alone, ensure that there is always someone on land to keep an eye on you, and someone who knows how long you expect to be out.

Dealing with sticky situations is covered in Chapter 16. But the overriding advice is simple - if in doubt don't go out!

### The seven common senses

This is the shorthand version of the health and safety briefing used by all BKSA schools and it is well worth repeating here.

Before you go out and during your water session you should:

1 Obtain a good forecast. To avoid being caught out by changing conditions an accurate forecast of wind weather and tides is essential. If sailing at a new location, seek advice from local riders.

2 Avoid strong tides, offshore winds and poor visibility.

3 Tell a responsible person where you are going and when you expect to be back.

4 Ride with others. It is more fun, and you will learn from riding with others, and there will be someone close by to lend a hand if you need it.

5 Is all your equipment seaworthy and suitable? This includes suitable clothing for the conditions, which may include a helmet and buoyancy aid. Pre-flight check your kite, lines, connectors and safety leash system. Check your harness and your board. Is the size of your kite appropriate for the conditions?

6 Are you capable of handling the prevailing conditions? Be realistic about your abilities and quit early if you are growing tired. If you are "pushing the envelope" of the conditions you are riding in, always make sure that there is safety back up. If in doubt, don't go out.

7 Consider other water users. Give space to others and ride considerately. Ensure you have suitable insurance this is an automatic benefit to all BKSA members.

In a nutshell :
**Check the conditions**
**Check your equipment**
**Check yourself**

Make sure you match your conditions and venue to your level of skill and experience
*Photo: www.extremesportphotos.com*

# Understanding the Wind & Water

Kitesurfing is only possible by harnessing the power of the wind, so in order to do it well, it is important to understand a little about the wind and how it behaves. Will it increase later, or change direction? Will the airflow be smooth or turbulent? Is there a spot that is better for launching?

This is crucially important to us, so the more we understand about the wind's behaviour, the better we can predict and make the most of it!

Wind is the name we give to a moving air mass. The air mass can be quite small or it can be very large. However, whatever the size, it has mass and is therefore affected by gravity, making it tend naturally to sink towards the surface. It also has inertia, and once it gets moving one way, it tends to carry on until something stops it.

## The big picture

When the sun warms the earth's surface, this heat is transferred to the air lying on the surface; the molecules become more active in their movements, bounce off each other more strongly and therefore take up a greater space. This expanding air becomes lighter; the pressure becomes lower; it can hold more water vapour and it will tend to rise. Any cooler, heavier air lying on water or in shade, for example, will now flow into the low-pressure area, and we feel the flow as wind.

Differential heating between different parts of the earth's surface causes this basic pattern, which may be on a small scale as localised thermals, on a larger scale as a sea breeze developing on a coast-line, or on a global scale, with trade winds blowing between permanent weather cells. Just to make this more interesting, half the world is in darkness and therefore cooling down at any one time, and the whole globe is spinning at 650mph. The result is that weather patterns can be quite complex, and that the wind, rather than moving in a straight line, will tend to travel in a curve. For our purposes, we need to know a little about the weather systems that affect our sailing conditions, and a good grasp of the features of a synoptic chart (pressure map) as used on the more detailed TV or fax forecasts is invaluable.

This topic is covered in more detail in Chapter 20: Undestanding the Weather. Our more pressing concern however, is: once you are on the beach, is the wind OK?

## Wind direction

Until you are pretty competent, have a rescue boat following you, or are sailing in an enclosed area of water like a lake, the wind should be on-shore or side-shore (blowing parallel to the beach) to some degree. For beginners, who are likely to progress downwind on each beat, a perfect side-shore or side-on-shore is ideal. Once you are confident of returning to your start point, some off-shore component becomes acceptable. A directly on-shore wind will be difficult to use, as you will keep finding yourself back on the

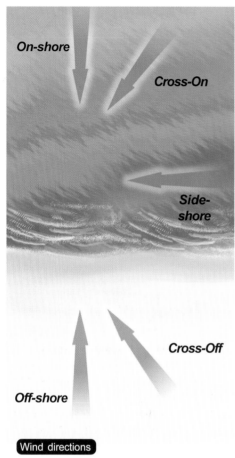

**On-shore**

**Cross-On**

**Side-shore**

**Cross-Off**

**Off-shore**

Wind directions

If the wind is strong, power will not be a problem, but maintaining control might be. You can try using a smaller kite if one is available, but high winds also mean choppy water, and if you are consistently overpowered it can be hard to learn anything useful.

The optimum wind range for beginners is 12-15 knots.* With more experience, this range will increase. The size of kite and design of board also have a bearing on the useable range of conditions.

## Wind consistency

The third variable is the consistency of the wind; those breezes flowing over large bodies of water like the sea are often quite smooth, but when they have been flowing over land, particularly high terrain like mountains or cliffs, the flow can be turbulent.

Wind behaves almost like a liquid in its flow patterns, pouring down over cliffs and 'rotoring' behind obstacles. Inland bodies of water like lakes or estuaries, especially those surrounded by hills, trees or buildings, can suffer from 'bad' air, making kitesurfing more difficult. Even at sea, if you are sailing close to a headland or an island, or even a harbour wall or a vessel that is upwind of you, you can expect the wind to curl around it and become unstable, with dead patches and gusts as you get closer to the obstacle.

It could be a bit embarrassing to be blasting past a ferry-load of admiring tourists when you are suddenly de-powered and start sinking! Try and visualise the airflow towards you, so that you are ready to avoid or make the most of any changes.

beach. An off-shore wind may be dangerous without a rescue boat, as you have the opposite problem - you will keep finding yourself travelling out to sea. It will certainly be a problem for trainees, as re-launching from deep water is much more difficult than a spot where you can stand on the bottom.

## Wind strength

The second variable is strength; if the wind is very light, it may not be possible to generate enough power to get you going, and you will keep subsiding backwards into the water as the board sinks.

*A knot is the standard measurement of speed on the water and is used to give windspeeds in all marine weather forecasting. A knot is one nautical mile per hour, and a nautical mile is about 1.15 miles or 1.85 kilometres.*

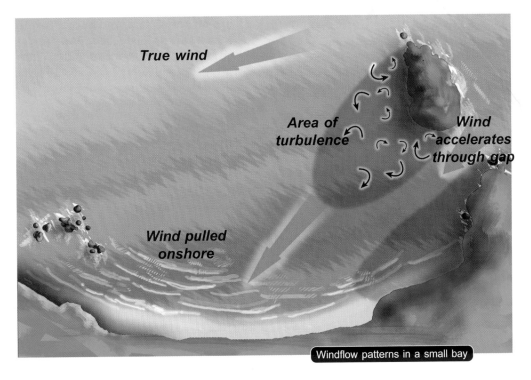

True wind

Area of turbulence

Wind accelerates through gap

Wind pulled onshore

Windflow patterns in a small bay

Unstable air with convection currents (thermals) can also cause gusty winds, and a thermic flow is often characterised by sudden changes in direction, too. Apart from the character of the wind, convection is often marked by cumulus clouds in the sky, circling birds, and by darker patches of water where the thermal gusts ruffle the surface.

Approaching weather fronts and squalls can also change the strength and character of the wind in just a few minutes. As a rule of thumb, if the wind speed is varying by 100% or more in less than 3 minutes, it is going to feel very rough, and it may prove very hard to keep good control. A wind speed indicator is a handy tool to help you make this kind of judgment.

Wind assessment is important when you are choosing your start point; a cross-shore wind may well mean that parts of the beach are in turbulent air or wind-shadow from a nearby hillside or headland.

Airflow over the landscape

## Tides & Rips

### Tides

Another extremely useful piece of information you will need if sailing on the coast is the state of the tide.

Tide tables can usually be purchased locally from a chandler's or harbour master's office, on the internet, or checked by phone with your local windsurf or kitesurf shop – this information is also given on some automatic weather station readouts.

The time of the highest tide moves back by roughly three-quarters of an hour each day, and a complete cycle from high tide to high tide takes around six hours.

This means that if you sail a certain beach at low tide at 12am one Sunday, and go back at the same time the following Saturday, you can expect to find that the tide will be close to its highest.

Tides are caused by the gravitational effect of the moon and sun distorting the surface of the sea. Large bodies of water, like the Atlantic or Pacific oceans, have moderate tidal ranges, but smaller bodies, such as the Mediterranean or the Red Sea, have only a small range. The biggest ranges are found when a smaller sea is connected to a larger ocean (the North sea, for example). In these cases the tidal flow resonates with the larger body of water, but in a confined area, and the resulting tidal range can be very large.

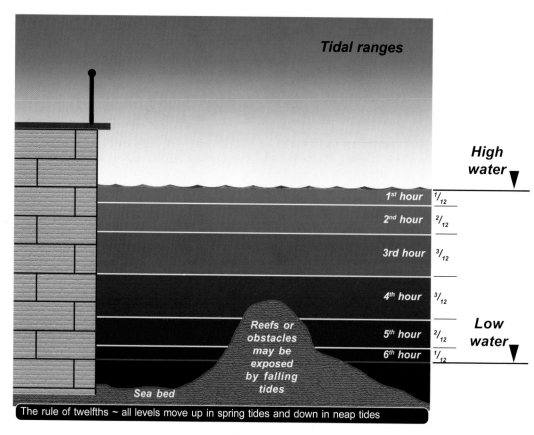

*Tidal ranges*

**High water** ▼

| | |
|---|---|
| 1st hour | $^{1}/_{12}$ |
| 2nd hour | $^{2}/_{12}$ |
| 3rd hour | $^{3}/_{12}$ |
| 4th hour | $^{3}/_{12}$ |
| 5th hour | $^{2}/_{12}$ |
| 6th hour | $^{1}/_{12}$ |

**Low water** ▼

Reefs or obstacles may be exposed by falling tides

Sea bed

The rule of twelfths ~ all levels move up in spring tides and down in neap tides

The tides are caused by the sun, and the variations in tidal height are affected by the moon phase. The highest tides are caused when the moon, earth and sun are all lined up on one axis.

These are known as spring tides (even though they do not occur only in spring!).

When the moon is at right-angles to the earth-sun axis, the tidal ranges are at their lowest, and these are known as neap tides.

A kitesurfer normally moves relatively fast and has only a small wetted area affected by the motion of the water, but the tide is still an important consideration to all sailors, for a number of reasons. A falling tide means that hazards like submerged rocks can change from being unimportant to dangerous in the space of half an hour; beaches can disappear completely; the condition of the water and waves at the shoreline can also change significantly.

If the wind is light and you are only moving slowly, an ebbing tide can be dangerous, as it can move you offshore at a significant speed.

Tides are not just the rising and falling of the water level – they are also responsible for tidal streams, which can travel at speeds of several knots along the coastline.

The tide can also affect the wind; a strong ebbing tide can weaken an onshore wind.

On many beaches, especially those with a steep or varying angle of slope, the state of the tide can have a huge bearing on the state of the waves and water. Tumbling waves or rips on the steeper shore at high tide may affect a beach that is easy to start from at low tide.

## Rips

A rip is a defined current that usually follows a channel on the sea bed and acts like a river, draining the water from the waves and tides back out to sea, sometimes at surprising speed. Rips are hard to identify, and you may sail right over them many times without problems, only discovering the drift out to sea when you have fallen off your board or the wind has dropped.

Because a rip is effectively a defined current, the best way to escape from one is not to try and swim or sail directly against it, but to move sideways until you are free of its influence before trying to come ashore. In these situations it is important to stay with your kit, as waves and rips can soon separate you from the board - which is bad news for you and for your gear.

On beaches protected by a reef, the sheltered lagoon often gives excellent flat water blasting conditions, but the water entering the bay as the waves break over the reef has to escape somewhere. There is often a narrow and quite powerful rip flowing outward through a gap or channel in the reef. Always treat such areas with great caution.

If riding a new beach it is always worth getting local advice on the conditions.

If you do find yourself coming in to land in an area of turbulent water, broken waves or strong rips and backwashes from waves, take some time to plan your approach, and time your landing between sets of waves; if necessary sail away to a friendlier spot to come in.

Always get yourself and your kit out of the water quickly.

In certain areas, such as estuaries, the tide state can create strong on-shore, long-shore or off-shore drifts. This can make the difference between safe, enjoyable sailing or struggling to tack upwind a long way. The well-informed sailor can sometimes use these currents to his advantage in making progress upwind.

The difference between a safe and enjoyable kitesurfing session and a nightmare of struggling for control can easily be down to your assessment of the conditions, so it is worth your while to check the forecasts, be careful, and quit if it feels too much for you.

# Setting Up and Launching the Kite

## Introduction to the kite

Before you even think of launching your kite, you need to check that there are no obstacles immediately downwind and that there are no overhead cables or power lines in the vicinity. A clear 'cone' of airspace at least 200m in length downwind of your spot is necessary to ensure you can abort a launch if it should all go wrong! You need to be aware of the weather (a forecast is very useful) and check the wind strength and direction to make sure you are in the right spot and are choosing the right kite.

It is very important to ensure that there are no people or animals within range of your kite lines. When you have made sure the launch area is appropriate and safe, you are ready to set up your gear for launch.

Lay out your kite on its back, with the trailing edge facing the wind. You will need to put some sand or other weight on the kite to hold it still - many riders

use plastic bottles full of sand or water if there is nothing suitable at the launch point.

Check that the bridle lines (those attached permanently to the kite) are tangle-free.

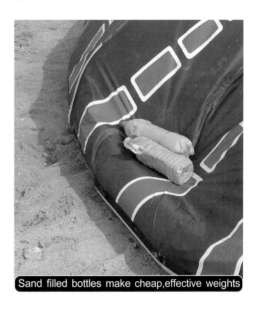
Sand filled bottles make cheap,effective weights

## Preparing the kite

### Inflatable kites

Inflatable kites must, of course, be pumped up; the best way to do this is to start with the ribs and leave the leading edge spar until last. This is not critical, but on many kites the valves are tucked in close to the main spar which, when inflated, may make access difficult, especially if they need to be pinched closed with one hand while the caps are inserted with the other.

Setting up. *(Photo: Tracey Kraft, Cabrinha)*

29

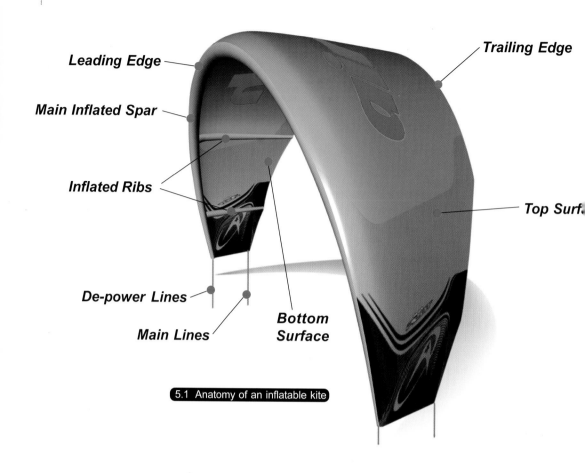

Leading Edge

Main Inflated Spar

Inflated Ribs

De-power Lines

Main Lines

Bottom Surface

Trailing Edge

Top Surf.

5.1 Anatomy of an inflatable kite

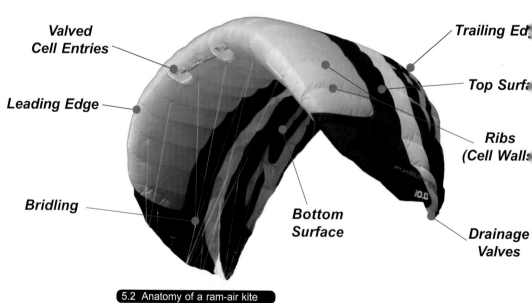

Valved Cell Entries

Leading Edge

Bridling

Bottom Surface

Trailing Ed

Top Surf

Ribs (Cell Walls

Drainage Valves

5.2 Anatomy of a ram-air kite

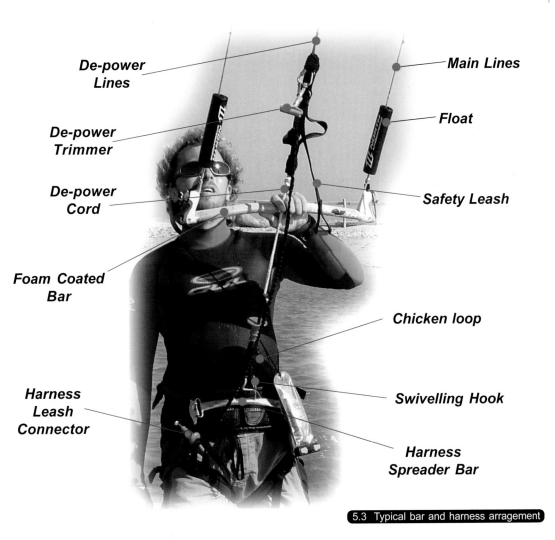

De-power Lines

Main Lines

De-power Trimmer

Float

De-power Cord

Safety Leash

Foam Coated Bar

Chicken loop

Harness Leash Connector

Swivelling Hook

Harness Spreader Bar

5.3 Typical bar and harness arragement

Sadly, quite a few of the inflatable kites have ineffective one-way valves; if yours suffers from this failing, you need to perfect the art of nipping them closed as you whip out the pump nozzle. The main spar valves are sometimes deliberately valve-free so that they can be let down quickly in the water if necessary. A better system is to have one valved inflation point and another separate deflation nozzle located near a wing tip. Make sure this dump valve is closed before you start pumping!

If your kite suffers from those annoying valves that release air when you pull the pump nozzle out, a useful tip is to use the big pump to fill most of the chambers and one of the smaller emergency pumps for finishing the job neatly. It is much easier to manually nip the valve closed using a small pump.

It is easy to drop your pump, especially the small hand-pumps, if you need both hands to pinch the valve closed and insert the bung, but if a pump gets sandy it can easily score the bearing surfaces

of the pump and in time will cease to work correctly. Setting up on a grassy area is the best bet, if there is one available. When pumping up inflatable kites it is important to get sufficient pressure into the spars. While a soft kite will fly ok, it will buckle much more easily in a swell and will be much harder to re-launch.

Many manufacturers will recommend a pressure and the better pumps are fitted with pressure gauges. A rough guide is that the ribs should be at around 10psi and the main spar a little less, at perhaps 6-8psi. (The manual will give details for your kite.) A few kites have a single-valve inflation system, so that the whole thing is blown up through one point. The downside is that it is a much bigger problem if a bladder is punctured, as they are all interlinked.

Wind Direction

Pump with pressure guage

As the main spar is filled and the kite takes shape it will be much more prone to catch the wind and fly off. There is often a small loop provided near the centre of the main spar that you can use to secure the kite to the foot of your pump.

The double-handed pumps must be used properly; if you get the bearing surfaces sandy they will soon become ineffective, and they are quite fragile too. Pumping with one hand or standing on the foot plate on just one side is quite likely to result in a broken pump.

### Ram-air Kites

Quite a few closed cell ram-air kites have very effective valved leading edges, and as a result it can be hard to get them inflated (if they are too easy to fill with air then they are almost certain to get water in them if you drop them!). In order to get these kites inflated you need to hold them up by either the bridles or

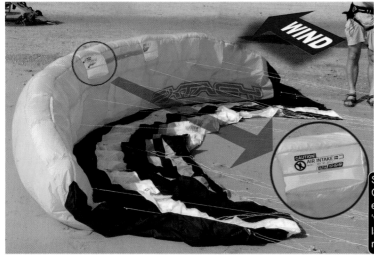

Semi inflated ram-air kite. Once the kite is rigid enough, it will sit in this 'wall' position until launched. Then it will reach full pressure.

wing tips and 'pump' them a little to help the wind get in.

Once part full, these kites can usually be launched and will take a few moments of flying to reach full pressure and efficiency. One note of caution here: most closed cell types have a velcro dump valve on the tips or trailing edge to help you deflate them. Do not forget to make sure this is fully sealed before you start trying to fly the kite!

## Attaching the lines

### Both kite types

Most riders do set up their kit with the kite downwind of themselves and the bar, as it will be when they launch. However, although this system works well if the kite is well secured (or held by a colleague), and the rider manages a good controlled launch, it is much less hazardous to set the lines and kite out with the bar end downwind.

This means there is no danger of a sudden inadvertent launch while you are sorting out your lines or getting hooked in, and if a gust does come and the kite starts to slide along, you have plenty of time to intercept it as it drifts towards you. Many riders and most schools use this method of setting up for safety reasons, only moving the kite downwind into the launch position when a helper has a firm grasp of it and the rider is hooked in ready to go.

The lines will probably be wound around a bar; if they are already connected to your kite, simply walk away from it, unwinding the lines as you go. You may find that if you unwind in one direction you will feed twists into the lines. Try a couple of loops, then stop and check for twists. If this is happening, try swapping hands and unwinding the other way; this will usually solve the problem. Having the lines wound in a figure-8 pattern onto your bar is much better for avoiding tangles than simple loops.

Be careful not to tug the lines too hard as the kite may escape and take off before you are ready.

'Milking' tensioned lines is much more effective at removing twists than trying to untangle slack lines. Andre is also using his body to help separate pairs of lines. ONLY do this if the kite is well secured.

Once down near the bar end of the lines, check once more that you have no twists or tangles. If you have, the best way to fix them is to put the bar down, walk back to your kite and 'comb' the lines through your fingers as you return to the bar - this is much easier if you can get a friend to keep some tension on the lines.

If the lines are not already connected, it is a good policy to simply pin them down somewhere near the kite without connecting them, and then unwind the lines as described. Once at the bar end it is far easier, to ensure you have no tangles, to walk back up the lines ensuring they are kept separate, and then finally attach them to the kite.

When laying out the bar, it is quite easy to end up with a twist in the lines, or sometimes with one de-power line behind a steering line. If is safe to do so, try applying a little tension to your lines to lift them clear of the ground to check this easily.

Virtually all kite lines have colour-coded sleeves at each end so that you can ensure you have the right one. Decide which line goes where and then stick with that system. The normal nautical convention is that green goes on the right (starboard) and red on the left (port). Many kites have colour-coded connection points which helps prevent confusion. You may have anything from two to five lines to connect and each connection should be made with a lark's head knot. This knot looks very basic for something that is so vital, but provided it is tugged tight, the lark's head has proved a virtually foolproof system. The harder they are pulled, the more secure they become. Never connect a line with a regular knot; it shortens and weakens the line, and after an hour under tension and wet, it may be almost impossible to undo.

  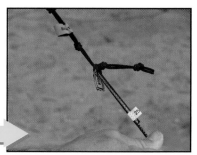

Knots must be made with the sleeved end provided; un-sleeved dyneema line has an unfortunate tendency to cut through itself under shock loads.

Most kites offer you short connection lines with a choice of 2 or 3 positions. This is a matter of personal preference, but the shorter the front (de-power) lines are, relative to the rear lines, the faster the kite will fly. The flying characteristics are discussed in Chapter 7: How the Kite Flies.

Once everything is connected you need to re-check that the lines are not twisted or caught on any obstacles. Once sorted you are ready to buckle up your harness, attach your safety leash, move the admiring crowds back to a safe distance and prepare to launch the kite.

Harnesses are available in two basic varieties: the seat harness, which has straps around your thighs and a slightly lower hook position, and the waist harness, which is simply done up around your waist. All harnesses should be on snugly, and a waist harness must be positioned and done up so that it does not ride up and put excessive pressure on the lower ribs. Harnesses, helmets and wetsuits are discussed in more detail in Chapter 24: Buying Your Own Equipment.

Deciding when to get changed into your wetsuit and harness depends on your riding venue. If it is a long walk to the sea, it is obviously better to carry your gear all ready to go. However, it may be more comfortable to get rigged in your clothes, then park the kit whilst you change.

Most wetsuits have a small pocket sewn in near the main zipper to allow storage of a car key, or you may prefer to hang your key around your neck on a cord. (Tuck it inside your suit or rash vest, or it could catch on a bar or obstruction when you come off). Bunches of keys are a problem! It is well worth taking just your spare if you are travelling alone (or if your companion is likely to wander off while you are sailing!).

Put your harness on if you are using one, ensure the strap ends are all tucked away, and that the bar is tight. Put on and do up your helmet if you are using one. Once suited up, it is time to launch.

But just before you do, always check:

- If you are using a harness, ensure it is done up tightly with any loose straps tucked away.

- If you are wearing a buoyancy aid as well, check it is correctly done up and make sure it does not obstruct your harness hook.

- The wind has not changed.
- Your safety leash is connected
- The launch area is clear
- Your lines are correct and not tangled.

Once your leash is connected, ask your helper to pick up the kite. Hook the chicken loop into your harness hook and ask your helper to move the kite into a position ready for launch.

If you are self-launching, make sure the kite is secure before you start to walk away from it. The safest position for a self–launch on land is with one tip folded over and anchored down with a few handfuls of sand. But if your helper is wearing suitable clothing (especially in strong conditions), it is even better if they can wade into the water with you and launch the kite from there. If you do get a massive surge as you launch, body-dragging a few metres through the water is a good

deal more pleasant than body-dragging down a beach.

Unless the wind is very light, all launches are best done with the kite at or near the edge of the window. This is because the edge of the window (Fig 5.4) will allow you to launch without fully powering the kite, and will therefore reduce your risk of a sudden surge. This way you can gauge the wind strength before you fly the kite through the middle of the 'power band'. It will make it easier to control and allow you to enter the water and sort out your board with fewer struggles.

If a friend is helping you, make sure that you brief them not to touch the lines and to stand on the outside edge of the window, or well downwind from the kite. This will prevent them getting burned by fast moving lines, should the kite launch unexpectedly - another reason to use the edge of the window.

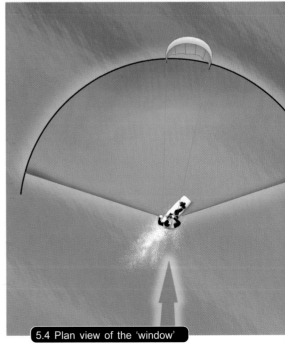

5.4 Plan view of the 'window'

There have already been cases of injury when a kite has been launched dead downwind on a breezy day. The sudden surge of power as the kite accelerates through the power band can pull you over and drag you, or in extreme cases lift you off the ground and carry you downwind for a nasty impact.

## Launching the Kite

### Launching Inflatables

Having put your kite in the optimum launch position near the edge of the window with one tip pointing into the wind, you may need to secure it, if you are alone, while you return to the control bar. A good handful of sand or small pebbles on a folded-over wing-tip will often do the trick. Do not use heavy objects like rocks, especially if there are spectators around, as the launch can fling these quite a distance and you could damage your kite dragging the fabric out from under them. The best advice is to try and get someone to help you.

When you are holding the bar and have your safety leash connected, you can commence the launch. If you are self-launching with a kite secured by sand on the beach it is simply a case of pulling the downwind (high) tip of the kite up into the airflow and the kite will move to the edge of the window and take off as soon as it starts generating lift.

If you have help, your launch assistant should stand behind and to the side of the kite, holding the leading edge vertically and pointing at the edge of the window so that it flies out of their hands. It is not necessary to throw it up into the air.

Common problems with inexperienced helpers include trying to launch towards

Let the kite fly out of your hand. Don't try to throw it.

the middle of the window or getting snagged by a line (particularly if the kite is outside the window as it may fly backwards), so any launch assistant should be well briefed before undertaking this task.

### Launching ram-air foils

Kites with closed cells for water use need to be inflated before they will operate properly (see above). To do this you can either allow the wind to enter the kite by holding it by the bridling over your head until it is half full, or (in light winds) stuffing the end of a pump into the cells and manually pumping the first 30% or so of air into it.

Having done this you can lay the kite on its back and put some sand on the trailing edge, or hand it to your helper before walking back to your bar to commence the launch.

These kites may need to be flown for a minute or so before the internal pressure is sufficiently high for them to work at full efficiency.

Obviously you must check that no people or animals are wandering over your lines when launching. If you stick to the edge of the window, and move the kite up the edge towards the zenith, the launch will be slow. If you start a turn towards the centre of the window, the kite will accelerate and generate power very quickly. However, the act of turning loses power, and if you initiate a turn too early, when the kite is only just flying, it will tend to stall and dive to regain airspeed and may impact the ground and spoil the launch.

In practice you need to 'work' the kite gently up the side of the window with small steering and de-power inputs in order to get it to the zenith position with as little drama as possible.

Ram-air kites only reach full presure after launch. A Peter Lynn Venom *(left)* and Flysurfer Extacy *(right)*

You can launch and fly a kite much more effectively if you understand how it works, which brings us onto basic aerodynamics.

Kites should be 'parked' like this and in windy conditions weighted with sand-filled bottles

# How the Kite Flies

There are a number of different kite designs available, but the basic principles of how they fly remain the same.

## Drag

The simplest type of kite simply catches the wind and pulls, just like a round parachute or a paper bag blowing down the street. Very simply, the wind pushes on one side and creates high pressure. If you have a line attached, the pressure trying to push the kite along with the wind pulls on the line. The larger the kite, the larger the dragging force. This is the principle of the basic 'diamond' kite used by generations of children.

## Lift

If the kite is carefully shaped, the airflow around it becomes more coherent and forms a primitive airfoil. All kitesurfing kites are of this type. The air flows in a curve over the top surface, and in doing so speeds up and creates lower pressure above the surface, as well as higher pressure below. As the kite moves through the air, the airfoil acts as a wing, and generates lift as the pressure difference tries to equalise (fig 6.1). Unlike a conventional sail that is static and relies on wind alone to generate this lift, a kite can fly back and forth at a good speed and is therefore able to generate a good deal of extra power.

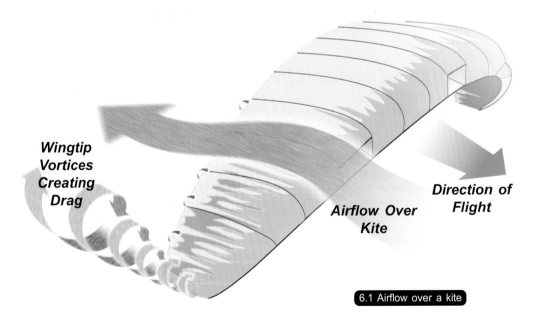

**Wingtip Vortices Creating Drag**

**Airflow Over Kite**

**Direction of Flight**

6.1 Airflow over a kite

The airfoil principle relies on the angle of attack being within the right range to work effectively. If the angle is too low, a soft airfoil (like those used in ram-air kites) will deform as internal pressure is lost, and even the more rigid inflatable kites will drop the nose and enter a dive with the sail 'luffed' (fluttering). This can be seen if the kite 'overflies' the operator and collapses.

Turbulent air can also cause a momentary collapse or 'tuck', though these usu-ally only last a second or so until normal service is resumed.

The other extreme - a high angle of attack - means that the air can no longer travel in a smooth laminar flow over the top surface of the airfoil (fig 6.23).

A useful analogy is a smooth slab of rock in a stream. It can tilt so far with a smooth water flow, but at some point the water will break away and create a chaotic mass of white water behind the slab.

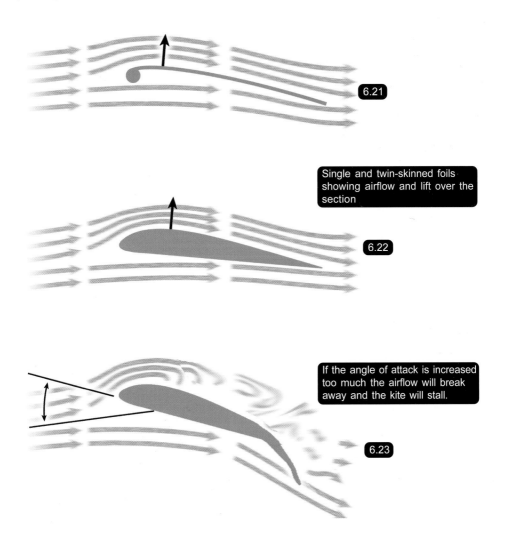

6.21

Single and twin-skinned foils showing airflow and lift over the section

6.22

If the angle of attack is increased too much the airflow will break away and the kite will stall.

6.23

The same happens with air; too high an angle (usually caused by over-braking on a 4 line kite) - and the airflow breaks away and the kite loses all power. If the situation is not rectified it will then simply fall to earth...

The manufacturers of kites set up the angle of attack to be in the correct range, so provided the operator does not overbrake the kite or change the trim of the kite by (say) lengthening the front ( de-power) lines too far, or the air become too turbulent, the kite will fly within this range and generate a steady pull.

Fig 6.21 shows that the same principle works for a single-surfaced kite and for a fully-formed airfoil section. These kites are now operating as true wings - if you were to hang a weight under them and drop them they would glide, just like a hang-glider or a paraglider. The full section airfoil with a curved top surface and a flattened bottom surface is more efficient at producing lift than the single skin designs, in the same way that an aeroplane wing is more efficient than a windsurfing sail. However, using a section like this for kitesurfing does have some drawbacks. A solid wing would clearly be the most efficient type, but not very practical.

A ram-air inflatable section as used by many kites is much more practical, but of course if air can flow in, then inevitably it is easier for water to get in as well.

Many designers are working on ways around these problems, and the latest generation of ram-air kites uses very effective valve systems to minimise the entry of any water, and one-way drainage valves to help clear any that does get in.

This type of kite does have a number of aerodynamic advantages, though they are more demanding to manufacture, and it is interesting to see how the designers of kites are resolving the challenges of building user-friendly but efficient foils.

## How the kite is controlled

Kites have two basic control mechanisms. The first is simply load shifting to cause a turn. This could not be more basic: increase the load on one side by pulling down on one line and the kite will distort and turn that way. Interestingly, when you do this, one of the first things to happen is that the lift is shifted to the other wing, and this encourages the kite to turn the other way. This phenomenon (known as adverse yaw) is most noticeable on kites with greater spans. However, the amount of load applied is generally so great that the kite has no choice but to turn towards the loaded wing. Control is simple but quite crude, just left or right. Even at 'full lock' most kites can only manage one 360-degree turn without hitting the water! Fortunately, the sport of kitesurfing does not require much finesse in directional control and the stability of these kites is actually an advantage when you are flying without

2-line kite on basic control bar

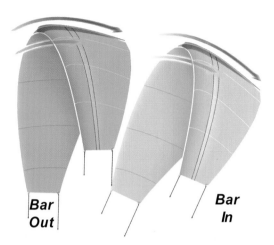

**Bar Out** **Bar In**

As the bar is moved away from the body more of the load is transferred to the front lines and the kite moves forward and adopts a lower angle of attack

looking at them, or with one hand (or none!) on the bar.

The second control mechanism is the de-power system. This is also quite simple; by moving the control bar either closer to your body or away whilst the front lines are connected to your harness, you can alter the length of the front lines. This way the angle of attack of the kite can be adjusted as you fly, and with it the speed and power the kite is able to generate.

## Kite control

True 4-line kites (i.e. those with independently applied control lines worked

Susi Mai rides without the de-power applied, the bar is kept close to her body (here helped by a static harness line on her bar). *(Photo: Peter Lynn)*

through independent handles) are rarely used for kitesurfing, though they are very popular for land-based power-kite users. Much more effective steering can be achieved by using the separate control lines connecting the trailing edge of the kite to the handles.

The load-bearing front lines can be used to steer in the same way as a two-line kite. The rear control lines (often referred to as brake lines) allow the pilot to pull down a 'flap' on one side of the trailing edge, increasing the drag sharply on that side. The kite will react very quickly by turning in that direction. If both sides of the kite are stalled simultaneously, the kite will simply stop flying and will fall backwards until the brakes are released.

This is a very useful safety feature, as it means a true 4-line kite can be fully de-powered and dumped safely at any time, without letting go of the handles.

This kite is stalled, as the bar is pulled tight to the harness, loading only the rear lines, and is dropping vertically backwards to the beach

At present these facilities are not normally available on inflatable marine kites, but the sport of snow-kiting is developing bar systems that offer the ease of use of a standard bar but with some of the advantages of being able to stall the wing or re-launch it backwards that conventional power kite users will be familiar with.

There is little doubt that more sophisticated and user-friendly bar systems will continue to evolve and to improve the sport.

## Types of Water Kite

### Ram-air kites

These are generally derived from those other flying machines, paragliders. And like paragliding canopies, they benefit from using their own airspeed to remain

4-line control handles *(Photo: U-Turn)*

inflated in an airfoil section. They provide excellent performance combined with easy use and are usually in 3 or 4-line configurations. They are almost unbreakable in normal use.

These types are very efficient and are the clear favourites for dry land kiting sports; the down side is that the cell entries required to inflate the wing are also potential entries for water if they are dumped in the sea.

Companies like Flysurfer who lead the way in designing the latest kitesurfing-specific models have devised ingenious valved inflation and drainage systems to minimise this problem, and a fully inflated wing may resist water flowing in many situations, hopefully long enough to re-launch it, especially if the user is able to use the 'backwards launch' facility that many models now feature.

Valved ram-air kite being launched backwards (trailing edge first) from the water.

But once a quantity of water is in, it is usually staying in, and as a result these kites are best suited to those who are confident that they will not be ditching the kite too often. Needless to say, a waterlogged kite a few hundred metres offshore is likely to mean a long swim.

They do have the potential to be the best and most flexible type of kite for the more experienced rider, and they are lighter and less bulky to transport (no pump for a start!). However, at the time of writing, it is still the case that most instructors and dealers are recommending that new riders initially select a lower aspect ratio inflatable model, and these still make up the bulk of the market.

### Inflatable kites

Inflatable kites are those which work by having a leading edge tube and some ribs supporting the sail that are manually pumped up before use. The single surface and the 'step' in the airfoil caused by the tube make them relatively inefficient as wings, but they have one major advantage over the other types - the fact that they can be re-launched from the water in a range of wind conditions, even after being thoroughly drowned in the waves. The original curved shape and inflatable rib design were patented by the Legaignoux bothers (founders of Wipika) and they have sold licences to a number of manufacturers who have either produced near clones of the design or are, increasingly, modifying the basic idea to produce a family of products.

Most manufacturers are also now producing 'bow' kites - those with an inflatable leading edge supported at several points by a bridle, allowing a flatter and slightly more swept shape in the air. This

Photo: Tracey Kraft, Cabrinha

idea is not new of course - several small manufacturers used the similar 'manta' shape for some years - but the potential for more performance and an increased de-power range has helped make this type of kite much more popular as major manufacturers have introduced new models.

Other manufacturers have made some interesting attempts to refine the aerodynamics of inflatable wings, either by altering the tube layout or by incorporating battens, or by hiding the tube inside the section of the kite. At the time of writing none of these have made a big impact on the market, but there is still huge scope for improvement, so it is just a matter of time...

A curved shape supported by inflated ribs means that the floating wing will always

have some part of the fabric protruding into the wind. This will drift downwind to line stretch position, allowing the pilot to manoeuvre it into place for a relaunch. Easy to fly and with slow handling, these wings are ideal for the first-time buyer, but because of their lack of flexibility in terms of wind range, a keen kitesurfer will soon need to buy 3 or more sizes if they are going to rely on this type of kite alone to give good riding in a range of winds.

Inflatable tube kites are available in a number of models, and, at least until the advent of the latest generation of bow kites, the trend has moved towards kites with mid and higher aspect ratios (slimmer shapes) as they are faster and generate more power. They do go upwind better, and while this is an improvement in terms of performance, it is unfortunately not true in terms of ease of use. Some of the larger high aspect wings that a rider might expect to use on light days are actually very poor at re-launching compared to their more basic low aspect cousins.

This is such a problem for the larger and heavier kites in lighter winds that some are almost un-launchable in the weak conditions in which they are most likely to be used. Some of the newer models are being supplied with 'reverse launching'

setups that mimic the characteristics of 'true' 4-line kites. Some have a 5th line that is useful for turning the kite over and making re-launching easier. These are discussed further in the section on control systems.

Despite this, at present the big high-aspect kites are still best suited to experienced riders.

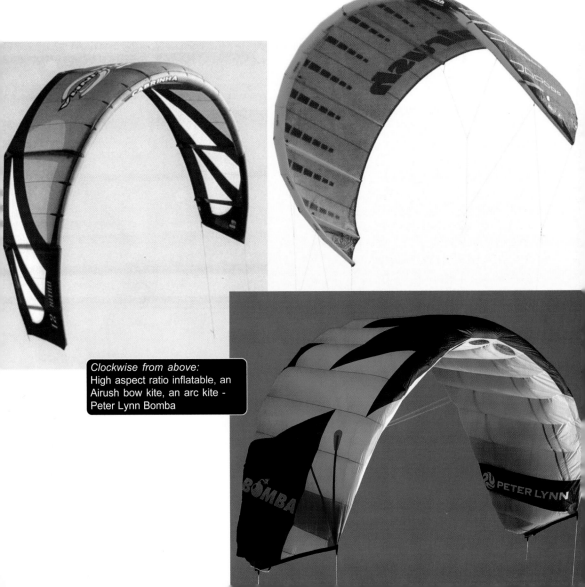

*Clockwise from above:*
High aspect ratio inflatable, an Airush bow kite, an arc kite -
Peter Lynn Bomba

# The Window

The window is the term used to describe the sector in which the kite will fly and generate power (fig 8.1 & 8.2). This sector is defined as pretty well anywhere downwind of the rider, but unless you are standing on a jetty, half the available area is going to be below surface level, so it is effectively unavailable to us (despite many beginners' efforts to prove otherwise!).

A stationary pilot can only fly his kite within this defined downwind area; however, when the rider is moving, the window moves with him.

The kite's speed and power depend to a great extent on what position it is occupying within the window. There are a few factors that we need to consider to understand how this works.

The drag on the kite is created by the wind. This is most apparent dead downwind; the kite is offering the greatest area to the wind in this position and so has the greatest drag.

Because of wind gradient (the slowing of the wind caused by the drag of the air on

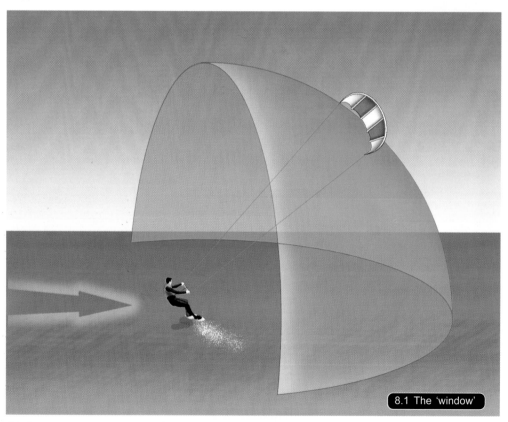

8.1 The 'window'

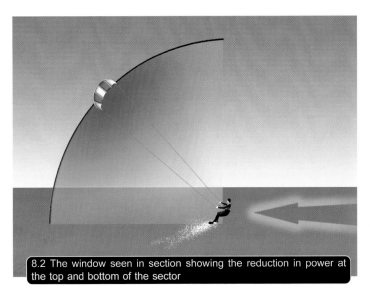

8.2 The window seen in section showing the reduction in power at the top and bottom of the sector

rectly over the rider's head) – there is little force generated here, as it is the edge of the window and the kite is likely to have very little airspeed, and this force is in a vertical direction, which can be good for assisting jumps, but not much good for generating any motive power.

As a result this position is often referred to as the 'secure' position, as it is a safe place to park your kite while, for example, you sort your board out. The width of the window is dependent upon the efficiency of the airfoil used, but inevitably, as the kite comes close to heading into wind, the airspeed drops, and there is less tension in the lines, eventually it will simply stop. If you do manage to get the kite outside the edge of the window (which can be done, especially on an assisted launch), the kite will simply cease to fly, or will drift backwards into the power zone.

This means that the total window is effectively one quarter of a sphere with you at the centre, a central sector that works efficiently - the 'power zone' - and a peripheral region where the force becomes steadily less the closer the kite flies to the edge.

The key to maximising power is to have the kite flying fast all the time to generate power from the lift and keep it near the centre of the window, to generate the most power from the push of the wind. This is not always possible, but the most effective practical way to keep the power

the surface), the wind speed just above the water is relatively low, so the best power is higher up the window. However, in the higher part of the sector the angle is poor, tending to pull the pilot up, rather than along, so this force is harder to use to generate foot pressure, and thus speed, through the board. The optimum area for usable power is around 1/3 of the way up the window close to the centre.

If you have longer lines, you can get the kite up into the stronger wind while maintaining your optimum angle, though this may make the kite's handling a bit sluggish. This is one reason why most kites operate on relatively long (30m) lines.

However, a modern kite is more than just a drag-producing system. It also generates lift as it moves through the air, and this contributes a good proportion of its power. This means that the window is much wider and higher than if it were just a parachute. The window extends up to its zenith at almost 90 degrees (di-

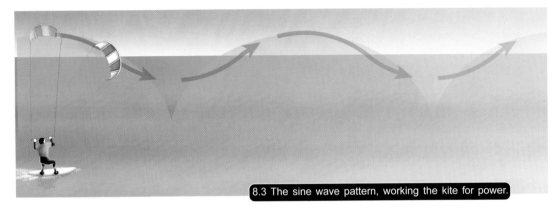

8.3 The sine wave pattern, working the kite for power.

strong and constant is to 'work' the kite in a series of smooth 'S' turns back and forth through the most powerful sector of the window. Because the flight path of the kite is like a horizontal letter S, this is often referred to as the 'S' or sine wave pattern (fig 8.3).

Perfecting this skill is the key to smooth controllable power and, to a great extent, making kitesurfing easier. If the wind is strong enough, you may find that the kite will provide sufficient traction power when just held 'still' at the appropriate point. A few diving turns to get powered up and the board planing properly are very often required before you can relax and keep the kite in a set position.

In practice, you will find that in order to travel in the direction you wish, you will need to vary the position of the 'S' turns within the window. This generally means being able to keep the smooth pattern mostly within the 'front' half of the window (i.e. in the direction of

When the rider is moving well, and board and airspeed are matched, the kite can be flown fast but remain 'still' in the middle of the power band of the window.

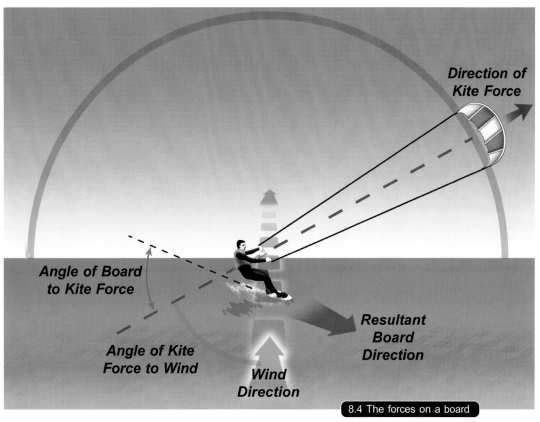

**Direction of Kite Force**

**Angle of Board to Kite Force**

**Angle of Kite Force to Wind**

**Wind Direction**

**Resultant Board Direction**

8.4 The forces on a board

travel). If the kite is allowed to fly too wide into the rear half of the window, the board will either slow down, turn to follow or, if well powered up, it may jump out of the water entirely! If it flies too high up towards the secure position power will be lost. If it flies too far ahead to the edge of the window, the board will either try to follow, and stall as it turns upwind, or simply lose power until the kite is brought back into the power zone. The BKSA training programme includes plenty of practice at using the window effectively. If the kite can be worked smoothly in the correct sector, the power will be much easier to handle, and the rider will fall off their board a lot less often than one who is constantly changing direction and where the power is very

'on-off' in nature.

The ability of the kite to fly at an angle to the direction of the wind is crucial, as it allows the wind power to be vectored by as much as 30-40 degrees from the directly downwind course (fig 8.4). The shape of the board allows this power to be vectored by another 60-70 degrees, resulting in a course that is more than 90 degrees from the wind direction, giving a slightly upwind direction of travel. This is illustrated in fig 8.4 and is explained in more detail in Chapter 17: The Points of Sailing

The sine wave or 'S' pattern works well if there is sufficient power, generating a good pull on the 'dive' portion and a reduced pull as the kite is slowed and starts to climb again, giving a rather stop-start character to your progress. In light winds it is common to see riders semi-submerging their boards as the power drops, then getting heaved upwards and forwards as it surges again. The key is to have sufficient power, which means enough wind and a big enough kite. Aggressive working of the kite and choosing a slightly more downwind course can also help. And it is worth knowing that a bigger board will keep planing longer than a small one, and a flatter board will retain power longer than a steeply angled one.

One effective ploy to get a good sustained pull is to abandon the sine pattern and go for a full 360 degree rotation of the kite in the window (a kite loop). This avoids the kite slowing down at all in the way associated with a sine pattern, and gives a long hard pull. The lines will of course become twisted around each other, and possibly the leash as well. When you want to untwist the lines, the kite's whole direction will have to be reversed.

This technique is best used on outfits that have a swivel built in and allow you to remove twists by spinning the bar.

Being aware of the kite's position in the window and its speed allows the rider to gauge the potential energy available to him; this is important if you are planning a big jump or simply deciding on taking a more upwind course.

# Kite Control Systems

## Inflatable kites

Inflatable tube marine kites are typically set up with a pair of lines connected to the trailing edge (rear) of the kite at each tip. These lines usually have only a very small facility of any adjustment, and are connected to each end of the control bar.

Another pair of lines is attached to the leading edge at each tip. These de-power lines are connected together somewhere along their length and the combined single line continues through a hole or a fitting in the centre of the bar terminating in the small 'chicken' loop that is attached to the riders harness. The length of this pair of lines can be varied in comparison to the rear lines by moving the bar towards or away from the rider, and they usually feature a trim adjuster that can be used to adjust and lock the available range according to the riders' preference or conditions.

The relative lengths of these two pairs of lines determine the angle of attack the kite will fly at, and so its speed and power, and to some degree the available width of the window.

Some of the 'bow' kite models have the de-power lines attached to a simple bri-

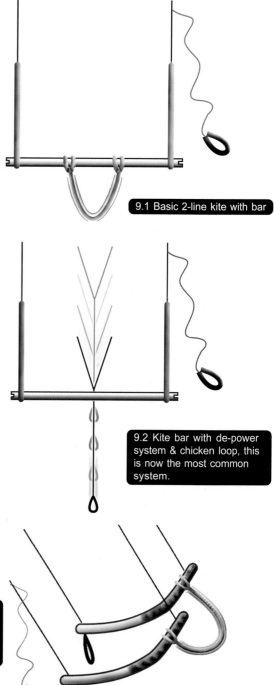

9.1 Basic 2-line kite with bar

9.2 Kite bar with de-power system & chicken loop, this is now the most common system.

9.3 True 4 line control system on handles, this set up allows very precise control, but as it needs two hands at all times, is mostly favoured by land-based kite flyers.

53

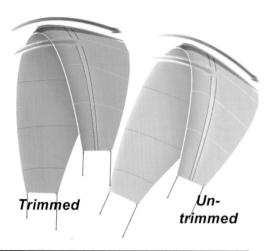

**Trimmed**          **Un-trimmed**

Trimmed de-power systems allow the rider to shorten the de-power lines, lowering the angle of attack of the kite and reducing the lift and therefore the power, especially when the kite is static. Paradoxically, when the kite is flying faster, this can increase the power generated.

dle near the kite which distributes the load to a number of point along the kites' leading edge - see below. This gives the kite a flatter and more efficient profile and also allows the kite to be more effectively de-powered, increasing the speed range.

## Ram-air kites

Ram-air inflatable kites are supported not by tubes but simply by their internal air pressure. Some, like the Peter Lynn models use the same system as the inflatable tube kites with 4 attachments, allowing the kite to form a natural arc shape. Other designs like the Flysurfer range choose to support and control the shape of the kite in order to flatten the curve, and these models use a more complex bridle system with many attachment points (similar to a paraglider) in order to achieve this. This system allows precise control of the kite's profile and allows a much flatter shape, and like the bow kites, allows a significantly greater range of angles to be set.

## Harness connection

The connection to the harness is usually composed of a small loop of cord protected by a plastic tube to minimise wear - the "chicken loop"

Virtually all modern kites designed for water use, use a bar with the rear lines connected to the tips for steering and the de-power lines routed through the centre to a chicken loop as described. Some older models rely on just two lines (no de-power system) but these are no longer in production and are now rarely seen.

A short stiff piece of tube or webbing is used to lock the chicken loop onto the harness hook. This system has no moving parts and cannot be jammed by corrosion etc. It is easy to connect, offers good security when jumping etc, and al-

Jam-cleat de-power adjuster

Chicken loop

power set up, showing the trimmer incorporated into the front lines.

though it is very difficult disconnect un-der pressure, once the kite is down it is quite simple to remove. It does not af-fect the prime safety system activation, an essential requirement of any 'home grown' leash or safety set-up.

Kitesurfers have been dragged underwa-ter and into obstacles and there have been at least two fatalities over the years. For this reason all modern kite bars are fitted with an emergency release system. These are positioned close to the rider so

that they can be easily reached with ei-ther hand and are designed to allow an instant method of completely de-powering the kite even under high pressure.

There are many variations, but the ba-sic design involves pulling a pin, depress-ing a lever or simply pushing a collar on the chicken loop line away from you to detach the bar from the rider.

In almost every case, dumping the kite and totally de-powering it will be sufficient to solve your problem. After doing this you still need to be able to prevent the kite blowing away and causing a hazard to others, and in many cases you will wish to get the kite back under control either to pack it up or to set yourself up to start riding again.

In addition to the emergency release all sensible riders also use a leash system connected to a point a few metres up one tip (steering) line and to their harnesses. This keeps you connected with the dumped kite and allows you to recover it to either pack up or set up to re-start.

The nightmare scenario is that the kite is tangled with a large boat or a reef and you need to totally abandon it. In this case the leashes are connected by their own similar quick release system and this too must be deployed.

The BKSA (and indeed any) training programme includes a session on how to use these devices and all riders should be familiar with the emergency 'bang-out' procedure on their gear. It is no use having a safety system if you are not sufficiently familiar with it so that you can operate it in an emergency.

"Suicide" leash connected to harn at rear to allow handle-pass tricks

Activating the quick release mechanism

Wrist-mounted Safety leash in action. This is a practice but at some point in your riding career you will need to be familiar with 'punching out'

### 5th line systems.

As the kites grew ever larger and therefore heavier, it became a real mission to try and re-launch them from the water, They were hard to manoeuvre into position and even when on their sides, without a good wind getting them back in the air was often impossible.

A number of solutions were attempted, and most of them involve fitting a 5th line to give the rider some additional control inputs.

In some cases the 'extra' line was connected to the trailing edge to allow the kite to be pulled up backwards and spun to re-launch, this was moderately effec-

There is a temptation for riders who like to do a lot of bar spinning, or multiple spins during jumps to leave off these leashes in order to minimise getting tangled, but this is a bit like driving without a seatbelt... fine for most of the time but a big mistake when you do suddenly find it has all gone wrong.

Riders who wish to do handle pass tricks (i.e. pass the bar behind their bodies in a jump) need to have a modified leash attachment (usually sliding on a bar or line around the back of the harness, to allow the leash to move around their bodies.) This arrangement is commonly (but inaccurately!) known as a "suicide leash"

Using a 5th line system to re-launch a large inflatable kite backwards, not too bad with your feet down, but still not very reliable when in deep water

tive in some circumstances, (see water re-launching).

A more common design feature is to connect a 5th line to the centre of the leading edge of the kite, this line is connected to the safety leash so dropping the kite means it is fluttering down into the centre of the window. A bead or handle on the 5th line can be pulled to help manoeuvre the kite around more effectively and to pull it to the side of the window for re-launch.

5th line systems are helpful in some circumstances but of course there is more stuff to get twisted. Though the manufacturers have tried to keep it clean by routeing the extra line close to the existing de-power lines.

If the kite falls flat on it's back with the trailing edge towards the rider then pulling on the 5th line excessively can sometimes result in the kite being flipped inside out.

They are a useful feature, and can be very effective in aiding the re-launch of many models. You do need to be familiar with their correct use, either from the kite manual or with some coaching from your instructor.

5th line bar setup and *(inset)* detail

# Control Practice and Body dragging

You have prepared your kit, have assessed the conditions and launched your kite, and you know all about the window and the emergency drills. It is time to really harness its power.

It is possible to work a big kite on land and get dragged 'scudding' over a sandy beach. Some schools use this system and if the wind is offshore or the water is rough it is very useful, but the best way to get used to the kite is to fly it in the water, and that means body-dragging.

The author getting in some scudding practice

## Body dragging

Firstly get used to flying the kite - try to fly it slowly all around the edge of the window, without generating any power and holding it still at the window's edge. Have a go at spinning around beneath it, and twisting up the lines and untwisting them the same way while keeping the kite still.

Get used to re-launching alone. If you can do this by dropping the kite into water while you are still in the shallows, this will make it much easier to master the techniques of drifting it into the optimum launch position. The more practice you have with your kite in shallow water or on land, the easier the transition to riding on a board. Many would-be kitesurfers are keen to dive in (literally) and try to ride before they have adequate kite control. Practice is the key to success, so take advantage of light or offshore winds to get some done!

There are four primary exercises that are useful at this stage:

### Generating power

First is simply getting used to the kite generating power. Work it in powerful sine wave patterns across the window to give you a good long surf downwind. You will soon find that an aggressive pattern will give you a faster ride and will learn how much control you need and when to avoid clipping a wing-tip and ditching the kite. Of course you will end up downwind of your start point, so you will need to wade/ hike back up to the training area each time.

This too is useful practice, as you can experiment with using the de-power system, holding the kite low or at the zenith, and flying with one hand. If there is a choice, always try and hold the kite over the water as you walk up the beach; it is safer for you and for other beach users.

### Practice water starts

Number two is simply practicing the start. Put the kite at the top of the window and just to the 'back' side of the centre line, look the other way (as you will when riding) and choose a point on the near horizon to aim at. Dive the kite strongly into the front half of the win-

dow to maximize power for the start (this will pull you up onto the board later) and then go straight into exercise three...

### Working the kite in a sine wave

Work the kite in a strong sine pattern in the 'front half' of the window only. This should result in a smooth body drag at an angle of about 25 degrees from the wind direction.

After a few swoops, switch sides and drag the other way. Many riders find one side is easier than the other, so practice your weaker side the most! The point of this is to prepare for holding your direction and generate smooth power in the correct sector when riding. At first, you will be watching the kite all the time - try to spend more time looking where you are going and control the kite by feel alone.

One of the most common errors in new riders is keeping their eyes glued to the kite, so now is a good time to prevent the habit getting established - look where you want to go. You will travel downwind quite quickly doing this, and you cannot work back without a board so be careful of ending up a long way out in deep water.

## One hand body dragging

The last body-dragging exercise is to work the kite one side with only one hand on the bar. With your arm outstretched, the other hand can be used to act as an outboard rudder, and can massively increase the amount of upwind progress you can make. This is both great control practice and a useful skill in itself, as you may need to body drag cross-wind to reach a friendly beach or shallow water at some point, or to track across and collect your board.

Given a good breeze and good control it is possible to body drag almost directly cross wind in this way, though it can be hard work.

Again, most riders find it is easier to control the bar with their right hand than with their left. It is worth spending some time working on your weaker side.

Body-dragging is possible when the wind is too light to ride, so it is a useful safely skill for getting back in that situation.

When learning, you may also find that your beach has a good surf running, and riding a board is beyond you. Body-dragging in big surf or waves is a lot of fun and is very useful practice.

Body-dragging is best done in shallow water, simply so that you can stand up and wade back, but bays or enclosed bodies of water like lakes or reservoirs are also ideal. Do not get out on the open sea unless you are being followed by a rescue boat. If you do not know the venue, do check for obstacles like coral heads or submerged rocks etc before setting off, and of course designated swimming areas or boat lanes must be avoided.

## Flying on land.

If you are practicing with your kite on land there are a few other considerations.

Flying any traction kite on land can be great fun but can also be dangerous.

Power assisted jumps can easily go wrong as you swing downwind under the kite, and injuries to ankles are easy to sustain. If you should let go of your kite it can blow quite a way, and will not necessarily stop just because it touches down; it could endanger livestock, vehicles or people.

It is very important, therefore, that you have a good clear area downwind and a leash to enable you to perform a controlled emergency descent. Using a

Body dragging can be used to retrieve the board in the event of a dismount

riders prefer a wrist connection point for their leash when on land.

Choose your flying area with care, and be especially aware of overhead power lines or other cables, for obvious reasons. Always stop flying if dogs, livestock or people try to walk through your window (and they will!). A kite line can give a nasty burn and a 10-metre kite could lift a small terrier hanging on to it quite easily!

Thundery weather can be a serious hazard, as the kite and lines may attract a lightning strike, especially if they are wet. There is a legal limit to how high you can fly a kite in the UK (60 metres); this is to prevent a hazard to low-flying aircraft.

Needless to say, the approaches to airports or airbases are not suitable venues!

Using your kite for buggying, snow kiting and particularly for powering a mountain board are all excellent practice, and can be done even when the conditions may be no good for kitesurfing.

large kitesurf kite on land can have much more painful consequences if it gets out of control than it would have on water; do be cautious in your assessment of the conditions. Remember that the quick releases are situated near your harness hook and although you can reach them underwater, it will not be so easy if you are being dragged on your stomach! Some

The biggest single problem kitesurfers face is re-launching the kite when it is ditched in the water. It is worth spending a good deal of time learning how to get the downed kite where you want it and back into the air. This is easiest in

Beware of obstacles!

shallow water without a board thrashing around, so do spend some time on these skills before trying to ride out into deep water.

If there is big surf which makes using the board impossible, you can have a lot of fun body-dragging, the only downside is that when you are laughing it is hard to prevent water getting in your mouth!

Watching your mates cocking up is almost as much fun as doing it yourself.

# Water re-launching Your Kite

It is inevitable that sooner or later (usually sooner) in your kitesurfing career you will end up with the kite ditched in the water. Before you venture out on a board into deeper water it is important you have mastered the basic technique for re-launching your kite from the water.

The techniques for water-launching kites do vary from model to model, so ensure that you have read the manual so that you know what system works best for yours.

## Inflatable kites

### 4-Line inflatables (low aspect ratio)

These are generally kites using the Legaignoux patent system. Manufacturers include Wipika, Naish, Cabrinha, Windtech, Airush, North, F-One,

Flexifoil, Slingshot, Takoon and many others. This group covers the majority of models that you are likely to be using early in your riding career.

Before starting to try and re-launch your kite, make sure you have your board to hand; if you do re-launch and surge off downwind for a few metres without your board it will be much more difficult to get it back!

The commonest case is that the kite has ended up lying leading edge down with you looking at the undersurface (see picture series below). It is stable in this position and will not re-launch unless you turn it over.

If it is already in the 'C' position simply start at stage 3.

Oh dear! The nose-down position

Turning over

**1** Pull the bar strongly towards your chest, then suddenly straighten your arms to slacken the lines. (If you can walk or swim toward the kite at this point that will help too.) *OR* it occasionally works if you pull smoothly on one line, then suddenly switch and pull hard on the other. If your kite has a 5th line system the same effect is achieved by smoothly and strongly pulling on this.

**2** The Kite should flip over into the 'C' position (see pic below). By 'playing' the tensions on the top and bottom lines you should be able to hold this position while the kite floats itself to the edge of the window. As it reaches the edge a smooth pull (more on the higher lines than the bottom ones) may help it to clear the water and launch. Do not pull too early or it will turn over again and you may have to float it all the way to the other side of the window! The lighter the wind the more delicate this operation.

You will often find that by holding some tension on your de-power loop (i.e. pushing the bar away), the kite will drift faster and launch more quickly.

**3** If the lines are twisted, most riders find it preferable to launch the kite first, then swivel the body (or your bar, if you have a swivel fitted) to unwrap the lines once the kite is safely airborne.

**4** Take the kite to the top of the window before attempting to re-start on your board. You may find it easiest to loft the kite with the board floating nearby, then find your foot straps and restart once the kite is up.

**5** However, if the wind is very light, having your feet in the board and edging it hard as the kite drifts can help you hold more tension on the lines.

### High aspect ratio inflatable kites

These tend to have longer, heavier inflated main spars and shorter struts, so they are generally more nose heavy, and can be very reluctant to flip onto their backs and get into the 'C' position.

Subtlety does not cut much ice in this situation!

If you gather in a couple of metres of the

The 'C' position

Drifting to the edge of the window

Re-launch

The 'U' position

front (de-power) lines and wade/swim toward the kite you should get a good bit of slack in the main lines; release the depower line(s) and the kite should turn over. From here you can get the wing into the 'C' position and drift it to the edge of the window.

If the kite gets into the 'U' position lying on its back with the tips in the air, you must be careful trying to tease it over again; if you pull the lines too hard it may fold in the centre and flip inside out (a good reason to ensure the main spar is always inflated to full pressure!).

If the ribs are inadequately inflated the kite will lie flat and be almost impossible to turn over and relaunch.

## Valved Ram air kites.

These fall into two groups: 'arc' kites with attachment points at the front and rear of each tip which behave rather like inflatable tube kites, or those with the rear lines connected through a bridle to several points on the back portion of the kites undersurface. The 'pulling towards you' trick is worse than useless with either type of ram-air kite, as pulling the cell entries through the water is virtually guaranteed to get water into the kite. The procedure for a nose-down kite is:

**1** Ensure you are hooked in.

**2** Gather a couple of metres of the rear lines i.e. those connected to the trailing edge of the kite (one in each hand) and pull hard. The kite should reverse upwards out of the water and you will feel a big surge of power.

**3** If you are holding two separate lines, drop one line and the kite will spin round to the nose-up position. Release the other a moment later, and if you have timed it well, the kite will fly up. This system is very effective, and much faster than having to float your kite to edge of the window, so if you get it right you can be up and riding again with hardly any downwind drift.

'Arc' kite. This is a Peter Lynn Phantom

Ram-air kite being re-launched backwards

However, there is a downside. If you pull the front (de-power) lines towards you when the kite is nose down, or take too long to get organised and the kite's front lines are under tension as it drifts away, a ram-air kite will inevitably start to ship water through the entry valves. A small amount of water may hamper the launch by adding weight but will self-drain

67

once the kite is flying; if too much finds its way inside, it is game over and you will be swimming back.

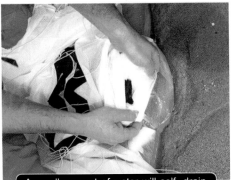

A small amount of water will self- drain, but once a valved kite is full of water it has to be emptied back on land!

## Kites with re-launch systems

Most larger high aspect ratio inflatables have proved almost impossible to re-launch in the conventional way, at least in the lighter winds when most riders would normally choose to use one. The designers have introduced several variations on the 're-launch system' theme with varying degrees of success.

If you have one of these, the procedure for your model will be outlined in the manual. Some may feature an additional line specifically for this purpose, or a kit that is retro fittable to improve the re-launch capability. (See Chapter 9, Kite Control Systems)

These '5th line' systems work in one of two basic ways. The first works by having the line connected to the centre of the kite's trailing edge at 3 or more points. This mimics a 'true' 4-line land kite with handles, or the ram air types discussed above, as it allows the rider to heave this

line, making the kite fly backwards up into the air. The theory is that a quick hard turn on the bar will then rotate the kite around and it will start flying. It certainly works on the land, where the rider can provide a firm pivot point, and can work on the water if there is a good wind, but the vertical space required to fly the kite in a circle is usually too great to be achieved in lighter winds, or when you are drifting with the kite.

Another design works by adding another line connected to the centre of the leading edge of the kite and routed through the centre of the bar with the de-power line(s). This is also sometimes useful, but again is only reliable in strong winds, or when you can stop yourself drifting (shallow water).

The fundamental problem when you and the kite are both drifting is getting sufficient tension to make the kite fly off the water. By pulling this line, and therefore the centre of the leading edge, the reasoning is that the kite can be manually 'dragged' to the launch point at the edge of the window and heaved into the air. Once clear of the drag of the water this helps the kite start flying again.

If the kite falls onto its back at any point and you then pull this line, it is possible to turn the whole kite inside out, a situation which is irrecoverable without help, or packing up and starting again.

In both types of 5-line re-launch system the safety leash is typically connected to the extra line, meaning that an emergency drop tends to be achieved without the kite spinning (as often happens when only one tip is under tension). This also increases the chances of a re-launch.

All riders should understand and practice the basic re-launch techniques before they get blasting on a board, where they will soon venture out of all but the largest shallow training areas.

There is at present no such thing as a totally reliable re-launch system for any type of kite. Most kites can be re-launched most of the time if the wind is reasonably strong, or if the rider can touch bottom to provide a solid pivot point, but in light winds and deep water no system is foolproof.

The moral of this story is that through the wind dropping, or through rider error, or both, it is always possible that you will find yourself with a ditched kite and no way to re-launch it by yourself. This is something you need to bear in mind when deciding how far out to venture. And it is a key reason why you should not ride alone.

x Pivec: Jeff Pfeffer

# How the Board Works

Deck

Adjustable Foot Strap

Toe Side Edge

Leash (Optional)

Impact Deck pads

Heel side Edge (Rail)

Handle (For Off-Board Tricks)

Fin Attachment Screws

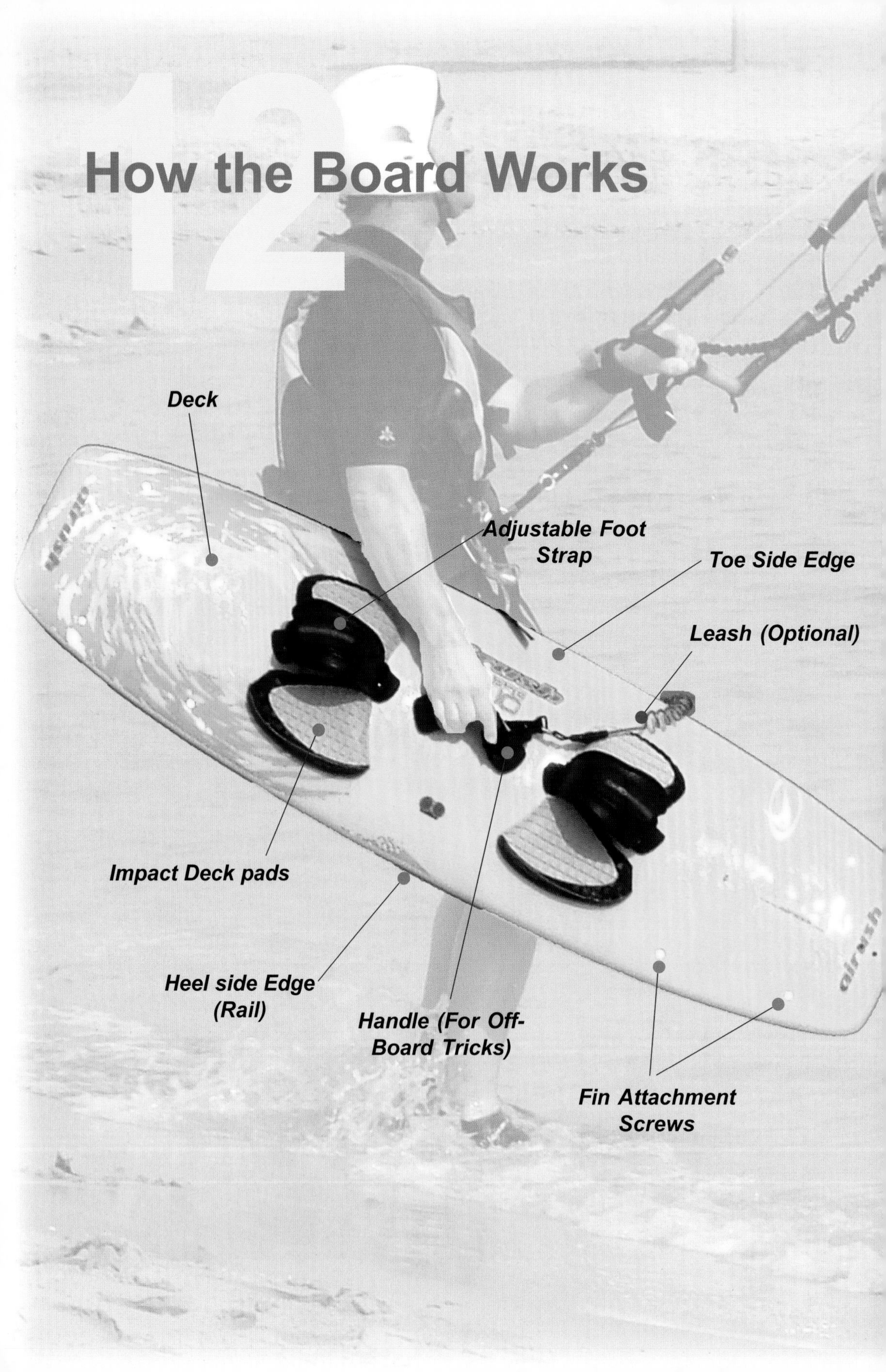

Kiteboards come in different shapes and sizes, each type having its own characteristics, as outlined below. However, the basic principles remain common to them all.

Owing something to windsurf, wakeboard and even snowboard design, the modern kiteboard has evolved rapidly over the short history of the sport.

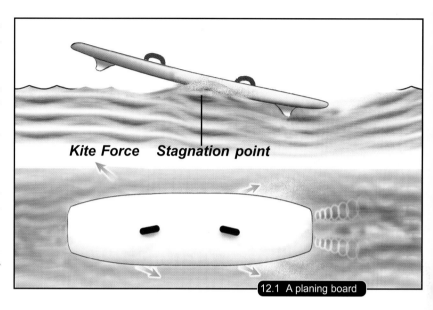

**Kite Force    Stagnation point**

12.1 A planing board

When moving fast over the water the board rides its own bow wave in a process known as planing (fig12.1). While a stationary or slow-moving board will not support much weight and will sink when a rider stands on it, a planing board generates lift as it moves along, and the faster it goes the more weight it can support. In fact, the lift a board produces is proportional to the angle of attack and the speed of the board squared. Or as I prefer to explain it - the faster the better.

The angle of attack is the angle of the lower surface of the board with the water. This varies with the amount of 'rocker' or curve the designer has built into your board, but is principally a function of your weight distribution. Too much power transmitted through the back or front foot and you can reduce the efficiency quite dramatically.

A common difficulty, particularly in lighter winds, is how to get the board onto the plane in the first place. A slow-moving board has a bow wave ahead of its centre of gravity (you) and the tail sinks as it is effectively trying to sail uphill.

The key is to climb over this 'hill' and start surfing down the other side. The summit of this wave is called the stagnation point, and a good burst of power is required for the board to climb over it. This may mean either pointing the board on a more downwind heading, or a strong and radical swoop of the kite, or a combination of both in order to achieve the plane. This is three-dimensional process, and the board is also acting as an edge, resisting sideways motion through the water. To get on the plane initially it is useful to flatten the board to some extent, reducing the drag created (once blasting you can dig in your heels further to edge harder).

Once the board is planing, the drag reduces significantly, therefore the power required to maintain it is noticeably less. The faster the board is travelling, the less area is in contact with the water and the lower is the drag.

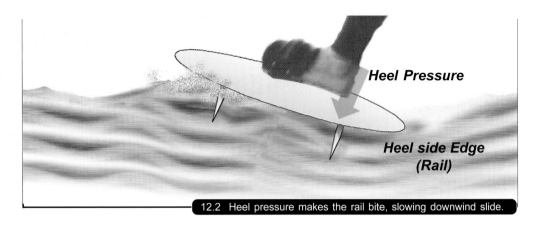

**Heel Pressure**

**Heel side Edge
(Rail)**

12.2 Heel pressure makes the rail bite, slowing downwind slide.

Windsurfers sometimes enquire about the volume of a board. In fact this is not relevant to kiteboards except in the lightest winds. Volume is a way of describing the flotation characteristics of a board - important if you are up-hauling a windsurf sail whilst standing on a board, but of no consequence when you are planing, and all kitesurfing is (hopefully) done on the plane. The size of board is really more concerned with the area that is in contact with the water and the manoeuverability. Except in the very lightest winds, rider height rather than weight is the critical factor. A tall rider needs a longer board, but a heavier rider does not (he just needs a bigger kite).

When the board is on the move, the ten-

dency - especially in stronger winds - is for it to try and slide towards the kite. By pushing the inner (heel side) edge into the water the rider can tilt or 'edge' the board and prevent it from following this course (fig 12.2).

**B**

**C**

**D**

To hold course A, the other forces on the board must be balanced. The kite pull, B must be countered by more we (leaning back), C and more drag (edging the board harde

Good edging technique

It is a similar situation to a bicycle on a hill, trying to roll to a point off to one side. Gravity is the motive force pulling it vertically downwards, but as the surface of the hill is in the way, the bike follows the easiest remaining course, which is to travel down the slope. To continue this analogy: if you edge the board too much, or try and point too far upwind of the kite, the power will not be adequate and the board will come off the plane and eventually stall, just like the bike trying to turn back up the hill. If you go with the kite on a very downwind course you will get a fast ride, but probably not in the direction you want.

If you do not edge the board it will still try and hold a course, though less efficiently, as the fins provide some directional stability. The fins themselves act as foils and generate lift which acts to prevent the board skidding sideways. This is good in one way and bad in another. Where there is lift there is drag, and the bigger the fins the more they slow you down. However, a board with a larger fin or number of fins will be more directionally stable, and will be easier to sail upwind. (Sailing dinghies and yachts can sail upwind very well, in part due to their relatively massive keels or daggerboards).

Kiteboards, however, generally use the whole edge of the board as a gripping device, so fins are usually kept quite small. They are simply there to prevent the board breaking away and spinning out as the lateral pressures build up. Many boards use 5, 6 or even more of these small fins.

A larger fin helps with directional control and provides a pivot point for the gybe, or slashing turns, and so is more appropriate for a bigger board. For these reasons only, larger directional boards that are also intended to be used in waves or as 'cross-over' surf boards have larger fins.

It is possible to kitesurf with an old surfboard (though both need the straps moving forward). It has been done with waterskis and even with a snowboard (although the snowboard did sink, which proved quite challenging). However, most riders will choose to use a purpose-built board.

## Board types

The author with a directional board

### Directionals

These are the original design of kiteboard, and the rocker (curve of the undersurface) and asymmetric shape mean that they can only be ridden in one direction. To reverse your heading you generally need to perform a gybe turn and change your feet positions.

They are generally high volume and are pretty stable, making them ideal for lighter conditions and for learners, and the shape

Directionals: Great for wave riding (Photo: Adva.

Board Types:

**A**    Directional, excellent upwind, for waves. Must be gybed.

**B**    Long Wide TT's. Ideal for first time buyer. Good upwind and early planing.

**C**    Short Fat TT. Needs to be edged harder, planes well, manoeuvrable.

**D**    Small slim TT. Sharp rails. Needs plenty of power. Very manoeuvrable, good for jumps.

offers good upwind performance and great wave riding. Windsurfers will feel at home on one of these! Some models are true cross-over boards and you can choose to go surfing on them simply by taking off the footstraps.

They are longer and have noticeable rocker (curved- up nose). This makes them far easier to use in waves as it helps keep the nose from getting buried. The curved rails (edges) and larger fin at the rear also make these boards much more suited to slashing turns, and pivoting off the crest of a wave.

Wakeboard with bindings

## Wakeboards

Wakeboards often have a short waterline and either tiny fins or channels in the underside. Boards of this type are somewhat harder to sail upwind, and will 'skid' more easily unless ridden at quite acutely tilted angles. The grippy shape and sharp rails mean that they can be controlled when conditions are very powerful.

Their lack of size makes them both highly manoeuvrable and good for jumping.

Most wakeboards have very little volume and are next to useless for supporting any weight. This means that they cannot be ridden in light wind conditions, as they will not sustain a 'glide' when de-powered at all, and are a problem if you do need to swim back to shore.

They are great for high-wind blasting and jumping.

True wakeboards are (usually) bi-directional and instead of using footstraps tend to use bindings. These can either be of the 'sandal' variety, which can be pulled

Wake-style board showing channelling (Photo: John Car

on with one hand and treated almost like footstraps, or true bindings which are very like ski boots and lock the rider to the board.

This is very secure, but it means that starting is quite a bit more technical. Not only that, but they struggle badly if the wind is gusty.

For all these reasons they are not very suitable for the first time buyer unless you are already a wakeboarder.

## Twin tips

Virtually all kitesurfers use now use a twin tip board. Usually slightly larger than true wakeboards, they owe a lot to wakeboard technology.

All boards are fitted with a pair of foot straps located symmetrically along the length of the board. This symmetry allows you to simply reverse course and lead with the other leg using the same edge of the board. Many boards are completely symmetrical, but because the board is

basically ridden on one edge, it is also possible they may be asymmetric along the long axis, and the fin arrangement may also be different on each edge.

The reason there are fins at all on the opposite side is simply so that the rider

Board Rider: Felix Pivec; Jeff Pfeffer

has the option to ride 'toe down' as well if he or she wishes to; this gives a greater range of tricks and landing options.

Some larger twin tips can be set up and ridden as a directional simply by altering the footstrap and fin configuration. These boards (known as 'mutants') do give the rider some additional flexibility, especially if they are wave riding, though they are not a different type of board, simply a TT board with additional locating holes.

Advice on what type of board you should get initially really depends on the conditions in which you will be riding. Directional boards with some volume, rocker and length are far better at dealing with a shorebreak that is commonly found on beaches with an onshore wind, and they can be used for surfing if there is no wind. But they must be gybed to change direction, and they are poor for jumping, so the turning advantages and conveniently small size of twin tips means that they dominate the board market.

Some boards are long and thin, others are short and broad, some have sharp edges and others are quite thick. On a more detailed level, the materials used also vary to give different characteristics. The more rigid boards are fast, but those with a flexible nature give more 'pop' which is helpful for those looking for maximum jumping performance. It is only possible here to give a broad outline of the features.

A long sharp edge is the key ingredient for upwind performance. Broader boards have a larger planing area and tend to be quicker to get planing. Therefore a good beginner board tends to be quite long and wide.

As the rider improves, the kites get bigger and the boards get smaller; a very small board is harder to get going in weaker conditions, but helps the rider control more power, and of courses is very manoeuvreable. The smaller boards are favoured for those aiming at big jumps.

Sharp edges (or rails) are good for grip when riding upwind and well-powered up; thicker rails are favoured by those who like to take the board off in midair for those all-important tricks. A longer board is more comfortable for a taller rider to adopt a good stance, and is easier to use in chop as keeping the nose up is clearly less of a problem. For this reason the shortest boards are usually a better choice for shorter or very experienced riders or those using very flat water.

Asymmetric twin-tip board

## Board construction

Boards are constructed from a variety of materials, ranging from PVC/foam sandwiches, fibreglass, epoxy resins, to carbon fibre, metal and even wood. The designer chooses the materials to give a combination of stiffness, flexibility, and, of course, price. There is no 'right' material. All production boards will be aimed at a specific market, so the choice should not be too hard. Custom boards that are made to a rider's own requirements are also available second hand, but are less likely to be ideal for your needs as a new rider.

Information and guidance on buying your first outfit is given in Chapter 24.

Any good dealer should be able to explain the pros and cons of each model, and match them to your needs.

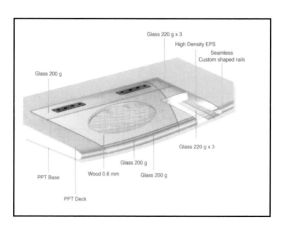

## Foot straps

Virtually all new boards are supplied with foot straps. These should be fixed in a set orientation - the actual position depends on your height and the size and model of board. The straps must be the right tension to allow you to get your feet

in and out easil your foot can get f and jammed.

Full bindings are u wakeboards, and w fective and comple ...c tney are such a pain to get on and off they are not popular.

You may come across a board fitted with 'sandal bindings' These are a foot strap with an additional heel strap, and are a halfway house between a conventional foot strap and a full binding. Sandal bindings were popular on several small boards before 'board off' tricks became common. Whilst they do work very well, are secure and only take one hand to put on (so you can do it in the water) they do have the disadvantage that you cannot whip off the board in a hurry, and if one foot does escape, the other is locked in. with the potential for a nasty twisting injury if things go wrong.

## Board leashes

There are some pros and some serious cons to connecting a leash to your board. The BKSA do not recommend their use.

A board leash prevents losing the board when you fall off, or are busy with the kite, and can also be helpful for handling the board as you get your feet into the straps. However, riding with a leash can mean the board keeps whacking you in the legs when you are not on it, and a long leash can be a huge hazard, as the board can get well away from you or easily surf back at some speed to hit you in the head or disappear between your kite lines.

Using an overlong (3m) leash was partly responsible for one rider ending up with

...legs tied together in coils of leash after being 'rolled' when he had fallen off in heavy surf; he was lucky not to drown.

Of course if you do not have a leash at all, the problems of being whacked or getting it trapped between the lines are eradicated, but if you do lose your board you may not be able to get it back. (Especially if it ends up upwind of your position and you are being drifted by the kite). This can be overcome with a good body-dragging technique. Students should master cross-wind body drags to get back to their board (which will drift downwind toward you in most circumstances).

As you improve your riding technique, losing the board happens less and less often, in any case. Ironically, the time that a leash poses the biggest danger is also the time they are the greatest use, when riding in surf.

Because of the danger of getting a fin in the head when riding a board with a leash (especially in waves), it is essential that any rider with a board leash fitted is also wearing a helmet.

There are 'reel' leashes on the market that operate in the same way as an automatic dog lead, with the spring loaded mechanism pulling in any slack. These are much safer than a straight or curly leash, and if you must use one then this type is the best option.

Never use a leash when jumping; the chances of losing the board and getting hit by it are magnified many times.

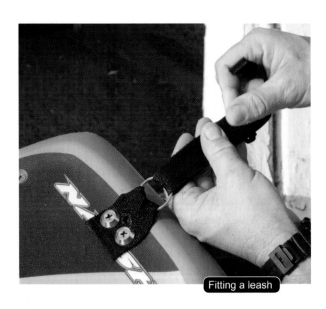

Fitting a leash

# Using the Board

By now you have mastered flying the kite, generating power, and controlling direction. You will have done some body dragging and a few water re-launches and know quite a bit about the theory of the window and how the board works. The next step is to put it all together.

There are a number of different types of board, as discussed in the previous chapter, but most new kitesurfers will be using a standard twin tip, i.e. a reasonably large board which is bi-directional and is fitted with 2 symmetrically placed footstraps.

This section assumes that this is the type you are using, though directional boards are also covered later in the chapter.

## Setting up the board

Initially you may be using a school board that is already set up, but at some point you may need to do this yourself. Before using a new board, you first need to ensure that it is set up correctly. This is best done away from sand and water!

The fins must be properly located and screwed in; they tend to be a tight fit, and locating the locking plates or screw threads can sometimes be tricky. It is very important that fins are secure, as losing one will be a serious problem on the water.

Note that fins can be quite fragile; remember this when handling the board, especially if you are in shallow water or near rocks.

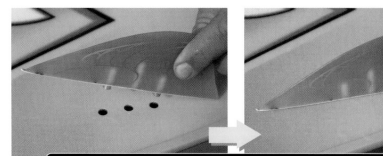

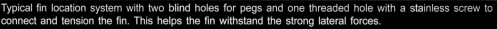
Typical fin location system with two blind holes for pegs and one threaded hole with a stainless screw to connect and tension the fin. This helps the fin withstand the strong lateral forces.

Avoid putting any direct pressure on them when doing up the bolts or screws. The ideal is to have some kind of trestles (as shown), but you may have to improvise!

Any anti-slip deck pads must be fitted, these are usually self adhesive and again any sand or water will prevent them sticking firmly. The foot straps must be set up so that you can easily push your feet in (probably whilst wearing neoprene

Most shops or hire centres will have padded trestles for set up and repair; this helps prevent scratching and sand getting in the threaded holes. If working on the beach or hard surface, lay your board on top of a board bag.

bootees). If they are too tight it is hard to locate them. If they are too loose your foot may go right through and you risk not being able to drop the board - a recipe for a nasty injury if it all goes pear shaped and you still have one foot connected!

Foot strap positioning is important; the spacing does affect the reactions of the board. Initially, it is probably best to locate them reasonably well apart, as this helps with board control and balance. The taller the riser the wider the spacing. Note that if you normally wear boots, but then are riding in warm water in bare feet, or the other way round, your foot straps will need adjusting accordingly.

Board leashes are not generally recommended, but if you use one it must also be firmly attached before you venture into the water. There is usually a fitting point for this on one end of the board. The other end clips to your harness. (Some older boards may have leashes with a velcro loop for connection to an ankle; however, it is easier to set up your gear, easier to handle the board in the water, and less likely to get tangled if you can arrange a connection on the harness).

It is worth spending a bit of time getting to know the board and sorting out your stance before trying it with a kite.

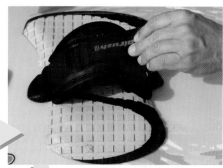

When you are ready to use the board, the easiest option (if the area and conditions allow) is to position the board where you will be able to walk or body-drag to it easily; then (using a well-briefed helper) launch the kite, either on the beach or preferably in shallow water.

Maneouvre the kite up the side of the window into the stable low power position at the top of the window.

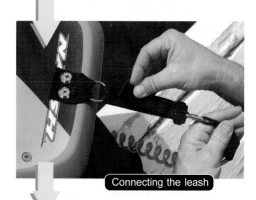

Connecting the leash

If the wind feels OK, you should now be able to walk or wade to your board, and keep control by pivoting the bar with one hand.

With your free hand, scoop up your board and (if you need to) walk steadily into the water, meanwhile keeping the kite in the stable position.

As soon as the water is deep enough to allow you to use the board without the fins grounding, you can sit back in

Raring to go

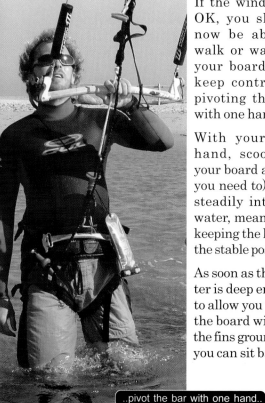

..pivot the bar with one hand..

Take care to keep the kite in the stable zenith position while you do this. The first few times you may find the board hard to control while flying the kite; an instructor or other helper can make it a lot easier, especially in waves or surf.

Board starts are easy if they are a team effort, so do not be afraid to ask for help.

Before you actually use the board under kite power it is well worth getting the technique and stance sorted out.

In the pictures opposite and overleaf, instructor Andre demonstrates the right and the wrong positions in a very useful practice lesson on a windless day!

## Stance

If the board is correctly angled and the load is 85% through the back foot with the toes of the front foot and the shoulders 'open' and pointing the way you want to travel, the first dive of the kite should get you moving the right way and under control.

The key points are:

the water, align the board the way you wish to travel (at, say, 60-70 degrees from the wind) and use your free hand to help your feet into the foot straps.

The easiest way to do this is to insert the front foot first, whilst holding the rear foot strap with your free hand. Then switch the hand to grip the back of the board or the central handle (if fitted), and use that leverage to insert the back foot.

■ **Let the back leg bent but keep it loaded**

■ **Keep the front leg almost straight and the toes and shoulders pointing the right way.**

This system also makes it far easier for the kite to pull you up onto the board than the 'locked knees' alternative, which needs huge power to have any chance of working.

## *Getting it right...*

**1** Keep the kite flying high but slightly towards the direction you intend to go. The board should be angled 60-70 degrees from the wind. 85% of your weight should be on the back foot. Point your toes and look in the direction you want to go. The back leg should be bent and the front leg almost straight.

**2** Swoop the kite into the power band, bringing you up onto the board. You now need to start the kite swooping on the sine wave motion, in the power band and in the area of the window in which you want to go. Do not allow the kite to come back past the direction of the wind.

**3** Once you build up speed, you may not need to move the kite so much as the 'apparent wind' increases.

### WRONG!!

The board is too square to the wind and both legs are loaded. When you power the kite, it tries to pull the board sideways through the water rather than up onto course. Huge power is required to get you up, and the result is often a 'superman' dismount over the front of the board!

This is often caused by pointing both feet across the board rather than having the front foot pointing in the intended direction of travel.

### WRONG!!

The board has been allowed to point too far downwind and the front foot is loaded too much.

Result - as the kite becomes powered, the board is left behind as it is not producing enough resistance in the water.

The pictures opposite illustrate common problems.

The top picture illustrates a rider loading both legs equally; this tries to push the board sideways through the water and requires huge power to get you up onto the board.

This is often caused by pointing both feet across the board instead of pointing the front foot in the intended direction of travel.

Even if you do get hauled up in this position, you will then almost inevitably get pulled right over the board.

The lower sequence illustrates another common problem for new riders; allowing the board to wander and point too far downwind, and again loading the front foot too much. If the kite is able to pull you, but starts to leave the board behind, you are in trouble!

Once you have your stance organised, the second imperative is observation: keep looking ahead, checking for obstacles and holding your course. Almost all new riders will naturally tend to lock eyes on the kite, so you will need to make a conscious effort to look ahead. This is where a lot of kite flying practice is helpful - if you have developed a sense of where the kite is without having to stare, holding a course is far easier. (If you ever look at photos of beginners, they are inevitably looking at the kite; the experts are always looking where they are heading (or at the cameraman!)

Thirdly, you need plenty of power to get you started. If the wind is strong this is pretty easy, but very often you will need a good 'swoop' to power up, then to go straight into a smooth sine wave pattern to maintain a good power delivery.

To achieve this take the kite (at a reasonable speed) to slightly into the back half of the window, then turn it hard and dive it through the power zone in the front half of the window - front obviously the being the way your front (extended) leg is pointing and your are looking. The surge of power will pull you up onto the board and you will start to accelerate forwards. As the kite gets low, take it into the upsweep of the sine pattern without allowing it to slow down too much or stop; keep your eyes forward and your board slightly edged and pointing on your course. Keep your back leg flexed and the majority of load through it to keep the nose of the board up. Easy!

Setting up the board

Initially you are bound to have a few problems. The board may skew to point up or down wind while you are preparing. You can use the kite to help orientate it again, but if you should turn too far you will lose control, so you have no option but to take your feet out and start again. The first few attempts are always much easier with a little help to steady you as you get used to the board. There is no substitute for an experienced helper at this stage.

Of course it is quite a lot to get right all at once (which is why a good instructor will break it down into simpler tasks and work on each skill separately before putting them all together). Things will inevitably go wrong sometimes.

# Troubleshooting

## Common problems encountered when first using the board.

### Pointing the board too far upwind.

This results in huge resistance initially, and a big surge of power to control; as a result you may either drop the kite or get pulled over forwards, and end up body-dragging on your stomach. If you do get up, the board cannot hold the angle and you either 'skid' downwind or create so much drag that the board submerges.

Start again, and this time ensure that your eyes, the board, and the toes of the leading foot are pointing the way you want.

### Pointing the board too far downwind.

The board accelerates fast, catching up with the kite and reducing the pull generated; again the board will tend to sink and you will soon find yourself well downwind.

This can be recovered by edging the board harder, especially with the back foot to adopt a more cross-wind course.

The same thing can happen if you work the kite through the whole window - make sure you are keeping it in the front half.

### Too much front foot pressure

The board will not follow the course you want, and either flatten out and head downwind as above, or, if you edge the whole board, simply drag through the water sideways after the kite.

Get that weight through the back foot (at least 80%).

All you need is a little help and lots of practice...

**Becoming over-tired and struggling to get the kite flying well.**

This is probably because you are bending your arms and hauling the bar towards you as you ride (or as you are pulled up).

This has the effect of slowing the kite and if it is not already flying fast will reduce the power. It is also very tiring after a while!

If you are working the kite hard but it still will not sustain you above the surface then you need more wind! A bigger kite, a bigger board or a slightly more downwind track may help.

**Getting catapulted into the air or being unable to hold a course as you accelerate fast.**

These are classic examples of being overpowered. You may need a smaller kite, or to wait for the wind to drop.

**Falling backwards at the start**

This is usually a result of not having enough power. A determined swoop of the kite and strong 'S' turns will give good power. If this is still not effective, try a larger kite, or aim a little more downwind.

**Falling forwards at the start**

This is a problem of balance and overpowering. Bend your knees more, fly the kite a little lower, and edge the board hard as you are pulled up. Try aiming a little further upwind. You may need a smaller kite or to wait for conditions to weaken a bit.

As soon as you are up on the board there is quite a bit to think about; not only do you need to keep the kite moving in a smooth 'S' pattern in the leading half of the window. You also need to keep the board steady in its direction and maintain your balance. The more you have previously practiced with the kite the easier this will be.

Balance is principally concerned with keeping your knees slightly flexed to absorb the bumps and keeping your eyes moving between the kite and where you are going. (You do need to glance around as well, to ensure you are not converging on other water users.) Because you are moving, the pressure on the lines is less great than when you are standing on land, and the kite may seem more sluggish to respond, so work it strongly to keep the power smooth.

A common situation while all this is going on is to allow the board to follow a curving course and gradually head up into wind. Once the board is pointing one way and the kite another, the next move is to get pulled off! Alternately some riders, anxious to keep power on, gradually head downwind until the kite is in front of the nose of the board. This also generally results in a quick swim! The board can only work effectively when the power is applied through your feet and the direction is somewhere between 20 degrees upwind and around 50 degrees downwind. For the first few attempts, a course of 10-20 degrees downwind is the easiest to cope with. The primary cause of losing your course is spending too much time looking up at the kite and not enough where you are going.

Once you are travelling reasonably comfortably, the board is producing less drag and you can relax a little and not work the kite so hard. In good conditions the kite's airspeed and the board speed are matched and the kite can be held still relative to the board.

## Beach starting

The beach start is a useful skill to learn. It saves time, keeps you pretty dry and is much more effective in very light winds and in surf, as you can avoid drifting after your board and needing to drag yourself out of the water.

Beach starting is simply of question of timing your initial swoop for power with stepping onto your board. It is quite easy with a larger directional, but is much more tricky with a low volume twin tip; for obvious reasons it cannot be done when you are using wakeboard bindings.

Assuming that you are using a direc-

tional board for this: just like a regular water start, place your front foot on first and lean back against the power as you dive the kite. As you feel the force taking your weight and driving you forward, step on board smartly. Do not worry about the rear strap immediately, as the main concern is to get the board accelerating, so your concentration should be on working the kite hard and smoothly.

Once moving, simply slip your foot into the rear strap for added security. Voilá!

Windsurfers will find this natural, as it is the usual system with most boards. The only problems you may find are grounding the fins if the water is too shallow, and sinking the nose on a twin tip as the front foot may be ahead of the board's centre of gravity. In this case you may need to place the front foot behind the strap initially and adjust your stance when moving.

This why beach starting a twin-tip board is very difficult.

Beach starting is most useful in onshore winds, as you can get an upwind line established quickly, but if there is a strong shore break you may not have room to get going before being 'waved out'. If this is a problem, the only real solutions are to walk around the bay to a better spot or get someone to help tow you out past the break line.

In strong winds or with a lot of lift, skilled riders may initiate a jump on the beach holding the board in one hand, then slip

Pretty soon you will be blasting with the kite holding position relative to the board - you can then concentrate on looking good!

the board onto their feet and touch down in the water just like a regular jump and sail away.

This is a pretty cool trick and not that hard if conditions are right. However, you do need to know what you are doing, so it is best left until you have plenty of jumping experience.

If you use a wakeboard or similar device with bindings, you have no option but to launch the kite after you have done them up and are on board. This is a little trickier, and almost impossible without help in a good wind, as you have to do up the bindings while controlling the kite and are very likely drifting as well.

Because a wakeboard is typically channelled or has tiny fins rather than having thruster fins or skegs, it is possible to 'skateboard ' over wet sand and straight into the water when you have sufficient experience. Be aware, however, that it may look cool, but it will eventually damage the underside of the board.

Wakeboards are usually favoured by riders who are quite experienced and who want to ride in stronger conditions. They are particularly suitable for those who want to get some serious air or do rail tricks.

## Controlling the board

Having learnt how to actually get up on the board we need to now concentrate on control when riding.

There are five major elements to board control.

- Maintaining your direction
- Controlling your speed
- Dealing with waves and chop
- Making turns
- Making jumps.

### Maintaining direction

This is often managed almost automatically by riders, particularly those with some windsurfing or other boarding ex-

Board Rider: Neal Hilder Photographer: John Carter

perience. The board reacts to foot pressure and the resulting changes in drag from the water. So if you press down on the toe (far) side of the board with the toes of your front foot, and flatten off the board, the drag on that side will increase and the board will pivot that way and swing downwind.

If you press with your back heel the board will 'dig in' at that point and the nose will swing upwind. As you practice this, edging of the board and steering will become second nature. The important factor is to keep looking where you are going. Two key mistakes are fixing your gaze on the kite and looking down at the board. It is rather like looking in a car mirror, or down at the gear lever - very useful at times, but too much may mean you soon lose your bearings and cannot hold a course, and can also make you a hazard to other water users.

## Controlling speed

This is done in a couple of ways. You can reduce the power of the kite by pulling it up into the top of the window; this works well and is safe, but it does mean you are likely to change course and travel further downwind. An alternative is to create more drag by edging the board harder, i.e. pressing the rail harder into the water and leaning back. This, combined with moving the kite closer to the front edge of the window, allows you to hold your course, or make better progress upwind.

If you need to add speed, this is best achieved by keeping the board flatter, working the kite fast and quite low in the window and by choosing a slightly downwind direction, if that is appropriate.

Photo: www.extremesportphotos.com

If you have a de-power system on your kite, the power can be well controlled by adding or removing pressure through your harness hook. The higher the angle of attack of the kite, the more lift and power will be generated. This is a big advantage of kites of this kind, but does make their use a little more technical.

The faster the kite is flying the more power it generates, so using the de-power system (pulling the bar towards you) may initially increase power slightly, but as you can take the kite closer to the front edge of the window, and hold it still there while you edge hard, it will allow you to cope with more wind.

Most new kites now being sold are fitted with de-power systems, though some wakeboard riders still prefer the simplicity of a 2-line kite, and there are still quite a few 2-line models available second hand.

Typically (but not always) the two front lines are connected to a single point somewhere along their length, and this line is connected in turn to a smaller loop on a sliding system in the centre of your bar.

The harness can be hooked into this loop (usually called the chicken loop) to allow you to alter the angle of attack to increase or decrease power. (See Chapter 7: How the Kite Flies) This system, in conjunction with good board control, gives a good range of options for managing the power and lift of your kite.

**Dealing with waves and chop**

Speed and direction are the critical elements to master, but dealing with waves is also important. A good rider will anticipate the water's movement and ensure that the nose of the board does not get buried in a swell by moving his weight

back as he hits a wave. As you plane down the other side, the weight can move forward again to maximize speed and prevent the board from stalling or spinning out. If dealing with small broken waves (chop) this is not possible, and the key is to keep the knees flexed and the nose of the board well up. If you have good speed you may find yourself 'chop-hopping', where the fins keep losing contact with the surface and you skip slightly sideways before re-engaging. Great fun, but a bit harder to hold a course.

If you are in white water in a surf break, the density of the water is much reduced (it is a mix of water and air bubbles). This will affect the buoyancy of the board and can make it harder to start or ride slowly. If you ride consistently in waves then a directional board with its larger fin, increased buoyancy, deeper rocker curve and longer shape offers a lot of advantages. Some twin tip models are "mutants" – that is you can place the footstraps asymmetrically, and using larger fins, can ride the board as a directional.

Shorter boards need good power management as they are generally less buoyant and are therefore less tolerant of lapses of power. If you are riding a smallish board in weaker conditions, the balance of maintaining power while edging for direction can be quite subtle, especially as small fins will keep losing their grip in broken water. This is one of the rea-

Good tuition, good conditions, the latest gear... what could possibly go wrong?!

sons that as boards get smaller so kites are getting bigger!

Stance is critical, and shorter boards will require a conscious effort to bias the load onto the rear foot in anything other than flat conditions. For these reasons a bigger directional board has a big advantage in wave conditions.

Whatever equipment is employed, a rider will soon get used to making small steering and speed adjustments as a matter of instinct. The key is plenty of practice!

Making turns is covered in more detail in the next chapter. Jumps are covered in Chapter 19.

# Changing Direction

A rider can make adjustments to his heading by moving the kite in the window and by edging or steering the board through foot pressure, but this only allows small changes. As soon as you are doing good runs you will need to reverse direction and ride back the way you have come. The method that you will probably use first is to loft the kite to the zenith position, subside backwards into the water, and then restart going the other way. If using a directional board you will step off the board, float it around to change foot position and restart.

These are effective but not exactly cool, and are likely to involve a good deal of drifting downwind. What you need is a quick turn so that you can at least get back to your start point or, preferably, make upwind progress if required.

There are really three distinct ways to do this. (And a few variations!)

## Switching (twin-tip boards)

The easiest method of turning is simply to make the front of the board into the back and ride tail first. In the early days this was a freestyle trick, but with the advent of twin tip boards and symmetrical foot straps it has become the easiest way of all to switch direction on a kiteboard. The advantages are obvious - no downwind turn means less loss of progress if you are beating upwind, and not having to move the feet means less chance of losing balance or missing a

footstrap. All that is required is to shift the weight from the old back foot to the new back foot as the kite changes direction. The board can remain edged during this change, so there is almost no drift if executed swiftly.

Most twin tips are quite small, so if the direction switch is slow they tend to wallow, and in strong winds you can find yourself inadvertently taking off if the kite is allowed to get too high. However, with a little practice it is a straightforward manoeuvre.

To begin with, most riders will find themselves subsiding backwards into the water before restarting the other way; however, the lofting of the kite to the centre of the window does give some lift that helps prevent sinking and with a good technique the rider can remain upright through the switch.

A few dedicated wave sailors still choose directionals, but for most new riders the twin tip board is the first choice, primarily for the simplicity of the turn control.

## Toe-down riding

In normal riding your heels are down (i.e. edging the board on the side beneath your heels). In this position your body is only slightly twisted as the kite is usually in front and to one side of you. However, it is quite possible to ride with the toe side down. In this position your body is twisted at least 90 degrees and the kite is to one side and behind you. To go from heel down to toe-down position you can turn the board but do not need to swap foot straps with your feet, or slow down like switching. This gives those fast carving turns you see in all the magazine pictures!

- Loft the kite into the neutral position above you.
- Pivot the board downwind and press down with your toes to carve a turn.
- Keep carving and let your body twist to follow the kite.
- Bring the kite down into the new front window position. (It will be behind you to some extent.)

You will need to continue to dig in your toes as you work the kite as it is easy to relax and let the board turn downwind.

To turn back is easy; just take the kite back to the original front of the window and follow it around with the board.

Riding toe-down feels weird, but it is great fun, and the position of leaning forward towards the water gives you an even greater sense of speed than being the 'right' way up.

There are certain asymmetric board designs that make toe-down riding impractical.

## Gybing (Jibing in the US)

### What is a gybe?

There are two recognised methods of turning a sailing craft: the tack and the gybe.

In other forms of sailing craft the nose of the hull or board can be turned through the upwind zone to perform a tack.

Toe-down riding

Under normal circumstances a directional kiteboard can only reverse its direction by turning the nose of the board through the downwind zone and therefore performing a gybe. (fig 14.1)

This does have a disadvantage when you are trying to make upwind progress, as the rider will inevitably find that they move downwind during the gybe, but on the plus side gybing turns are fully powered making them fast and exciting and allowing you to keep the board on the plane.

### How to Gybe

There are two variations of the basic technique: moving the feet before carving the turn and moving the feet afterwards. The second is perhaps a little trickier to master, but may be favoured by windsurfers as it is based on the classic windsurfing gybe.

In all cases the best way to start is to ensure that you are riding smoothly and not too overpowered - if you are edging the board hard or leaning back, gybing will be much harder. This section assumes you are using a directional board.

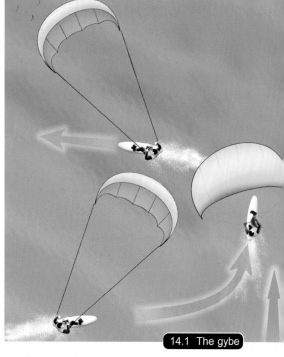

14.1 The gybe

### Feet first

Take your feet out of the straps and when you feel balanced switch your old rear foot to the new front strap (or more likely on top of it or next to it). Immediately move the old front foot back and place it next to the rear strap. (The kite should be moving across the top of the window at this point and the board will be turning downwind.) You can now carve the board around by pressing on the downwind rail with the new back foot. As the board comes round onto the new heading you need to complete the dance by placing the 'old' front foot into the rear strap, finish off by slipping the old rear foot into the front strap.

Carving the gybe

## Feet last

Take the rear foot out of the straps but keep it in that general area. Press with the toes of the rear foot to carve the board, keeping your feet still until the board is round onto its new heading. You are now sailing in the 'toe down' position'. As soon as you feel balanced switch your feet, then slip them into the foot straps.

While you are moving your feet around, the kite should be lofted to the higher edge of the window, and as the board is carved around pulled down into the new leading quarter of the window. The lift created by the kite minimises your weight on the board and makes the whole

thing more stable as you move your feet. Even if the gybe is a bit slow at first and de-powers the board, you should be in a position to immediately dive the kite and power up again as you complete the turn. Plenty of successful gybes involve a moment spent almost squatting in the water! (so I have heard!)

No words can explain the feel of the turn; each board will react differently depending on its volume and width. Like most things it is a question of practice - judging the right moment to move your feet, and keeping your knees bent and movements fluid.

Like most exercises requiring balance

and co-ordination there is no substitute for watching a competent rider demonstrate a few times and then just keeping on practicing.

Note: because you will be moving your feet in and out of the straps, they must be set with sufficient play to let you do this easily. Many twin tip boards have 'one way' foot straps designed to accept the foot from one side only, making gybing impractical.

## Variations

A very popular variation of the toe down turn is to hop out of the water with a very low jump and turn the board so that you are riding on the same course as before, but toe down. This is done seconds before the turn itself.

From this position you can then perform a nice fast carving turn in front of the admiring crowds, finishing in the heel down (regular) position and blast away. If your kite control is good, you can combine this turn with a full speed 360 turn of the kite (kite loop) for added speed and style.

## Airborne turns

One of the attractions of the sport is the potential for big jumps. This can be exploited by switching direction whilst airborne.

As the kite is lofted, it can be taken straight through the top of the window and down to the other side ready to power you away on the new course. This does take good leg muscle control to make sure the board is correctly positioned for the new direction.

# Kitesurfing With Others

Kitesurfing is a sport that takes up a lot of room! Most waterborne sports, like sailing dinghies, windsurfers or even jetskis, occupy a pretty small area of water at a time. Waterskiers and wakeboarders do, of course, have a line connecting them to the boat, but this is generally pretty much in line with their direction of travel. The tow boat can manoeuvre easily to avoid a collision, and both the boat and the skier are very familiar and very visible.

By contrast, the kitesurfer is connected by near-invisible lines to his kite that may well be at almost 90 degrees from his direction of travel. The lines are sweeping an area of the water surface up to 40 metres wide like a scythe. The kite itself is usually quite visible, though it can be obscured by a swell, but the main problem for the rider is that other water users may not associate the kite with the rider and can regard the space between them as clear water. Multiply this situation by 10 or 20 riders on a good day and it is easy to see how even a large bay can soon become a seriously congested place.

This is made much worse if the rider has fallen off and the kite is ditched. The lines will be invisible on the water and the rider may also be hard to spot in any swell.

A significant issue for kitesurfers is that windsurfers require very similar conditions and locations. In fact they are often the same people who simply choose their weapon according to conditions! This is good from the point of view that windsurfers will be aware of what a kitesurfer is and what they are capable of, but bad in that it means segregation is sometimes not a realistic option.

And there is the problem of conflict with each other; it is good fun to ride close to your mate, but if the kites or lines should become tangled it can quickly lead to a very hazardous situation. There has already been a serious accident where one rider was badly injured after having been dragged by two kites - his own and a 'dumped' kite that had been released by another upwind rider and been caught in his lines.

## Common sense rules for Everyone's Benefit

- Try and use a separate area, particularly when you are a beginner and will be likely to drop the kite.

- Keep a good lookout. This may sound obvious, but holding a mental picture of the other water users that you update every few seconds by scanning the area will help you anticipate conflicts in plenty of time and either change course or hoist the kite into a safer position. It is common for inexperienced riders to look at their kite for long periods and thereby increase their risk of conflict with others.

- Match your course and speed to other riders. Rather than running parallel to another rider, try slotting in behind them; this way you will be using the same sector of water as them and consequently twice as many riders can use the same area.

- The rider can minimise the danger area defined by the lines by putting the kite into a more vertical position. If another rider or a windsurfer gets close, lofting the kite to quickly angle the lines upward drastically reduces the potential conflict area.

- If you wipe out, be aware that lines lying on the water are not easily visible and cannot be moved out of the way; so they can easily catch the fin of a windsurfer or another kiteboard. You can minimise this risk by not attempting difficult manoeuvres or using new equipment when the water is busy.

## Collision avoidance Rules

The first thing to know about these rules is that you should never need to use them if you keep a good lookout and avoid a conflict situation arising! If you stick to the common sense rules opposite, the avoidance rules need never apply.

*The overriding rule is to take any action necessary to avoid a collision.*

## Specific situations

### Head-on collision situation

When two craft are on opposite courses, the international convention for all watercraft is that starboard tack has priority; this means the one leading with their right shoulder has the right of way and the other craft should take avoiding action. Assuming that you are travelling pretty well cross wind for this situation to arise, your only avoidance option is to bear off downwind.

Head-on conflict, A is leading with his right shoulder and so B has to bear off downwind to give way. Kite A (upwind kite) should be moved up and Kite B moved down.

### Converging courses

When two craft are converging, the one to windward (upwind) shall give way.

Note the use of the word 'craft' - you have the same responsibility as any other sailing craft to take action to avoid conflict. Strictly speaking the craft on a starboard tack has the right of way, in other words the craft with the wind hitting the right or starboard side.

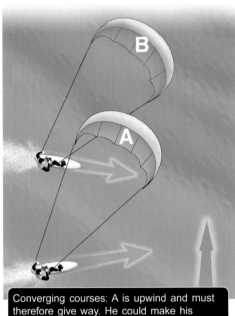

Converging courses: A is upwind and must therefore give way. He could make his course more upwind, or if not possible he must slow down and drop behind B. Again Kite A is upwind and should loft his kite while B moves it down.

### Overtaking

If you are the overtaking craft, you must make sure you have been seen and take a course that will give you plenty of room to get by without any risk of collision. If you are the craft being overtaken, you must continue on your course (i.e. do not make any unexpected course changes that could increase the risk of collision).

### Jumping

When jumping, ensure that the area you are using is clear of other water users for some distance downwind. Never try to jump physical obstacles such as boats, buoys, windsurfers or swimmers. Do not aim to finish a jump on dry land.

### Shipping channels

If you must cross one, do so in as straight a line as possible, preferably at 90 degrees.

You have no rights at all when you are in a shipping channel! Your only option is to ride defensively, keeping well away from other traffic or to avoid spending much time in shipping channels.

### Swimming areas

Many beaches have designated swimming areas. They are often surrounded by floating ropes or marked by flags. They are likely to have kids as well as adults in them.

Treat them as no-go areas and stay well away.

The same applies for divers (often marked by a small buoy) and dive sites, and for moored boats.

### Consideration for all

Always ride with consideration for others. Just because you may have priority over another craft does not mean you should abuse this. Avoid impeding their paths where possible. (These are safety rules - of course it is different in races, where using your right of way to your advantage is a tactical weapon!)

Apart from the risk of riders colliding, kitesurfing has the added possibility of crossing lines. The rule, if this is immi-

nent, is that the upwind rider moves his kite to the top of the window, while the downwind rider moves his kite down.

Windsurfing, sailing and many other activities are allowed in shared venues like lakes and on popular beaches because these sports have built up a good reputation for safety and consideration. Sadly some others, such as jet-skiing, are banned from many suitable locations, and to a great extent it is because of the undisciplined behaviour of some of the riders.

Kitesurfers are the new kids on the block and landowners, local authorities and others will be cautious about allowing access.

Asking permission, avoiding conflict with other water users and showing consideration will count heavily in our favour. We are all ambassadors of the sport!

# Getting Out of Trouble & Dealing With Emergencies

Like any adventure sport, kitesurfing carries some risks; these can be minimised by getting proper training - preferably from an approved BKSA training school - taking good care of the equipment, riding within your limits and particularly by exercising caution with the weather conditions. However, if you keep riding long enough, eventually an unforeseen situation will catch you out. Every experienced rider has a few 'kitemare' stories to tell!

The most obvious danger areas are being blown out to sea or being blown up the beach into people, rocks, roads etc. These can be avoided simply by choosing your conditions carefully and never trying to ride in an offshore wind without a rescue boat or an onshore wind without lots of space to dump the kite safely.

There are a few other situations that you may need to deal with.

## ■ You cannot stay on your board

If you are overpowered or underpowered or if the wind is just too gusty, at some point you will get too tired to keep try-

ing. If you can keep the kite airborne, you will simply need to body drag to the beach. Remember your body-dragging exercises - sticking one arm out will allow you to increase your cross-wind angle considerably. (Though dragging a kiteboard does reduce the angle to the wind to some extent).

## ■ Losing control

If you have lost control of the kite for some reason - perhaps it is overpowered, a line has broken and it is spinning or is broken in some other way - you may have no option but to drop your control bar and allow the safety leash to keep you in contact while the kite falls into the water. If this happens (especially in strong winds) it is important that you follow the self rescue procedure outlined below. This will prevent the kite from re-inflating and launching while you are trying to get it under control.

## ■ Serious problems

The nightmare scenario is that the kite gets caught on a moving craft and the rider cannot get loose, or is blowing towards rocks. The safety leash is always connected with a punch-out quick-release system or with velcro, so you should, if you have to, be able to drop it away .

If you are hooked in, or unable to get the lines free of your harness hook, or

Whoops! not what you want to see

have suspension lines tangled round a foot or board, you have no option but to cut yourself free. In order to do this it is necessary to carry a bridle knife on your harness and be familiar with finding it, even underwater. These bridle knives, (also known as hook knives) are perfectly safe to store on your harness with the blades hidden inside a narrow slot, but are very efficient at slicing through lines. They are available from good dealers or from parachuting centres. They typically cost about £10.

### ■ Equipment failure

If you have an equipment failure, or conditions change and you find you cannot get into shore by riding or by body dragging, your only option is to wrap up the kite and paddle to the beach. Follow the self-rescue procedure laid out below.

One kiteboarder can actually tow another if conditions are strong enough, but this may not be of much practical use for rescue, as the pulling board will be hard pressed to make any upwind progress (probably no more than you could achieve body dragging), and anyhow you are likely to have a half deflated kite to deal with as well.

### ■ Calling for help

If you need help, the international signal for distress is to wave both arms symmetrically from the water line to above your head. If you are OK, the signal is to place one hand on your head. Be very careful in calling a vessel to your aid, as the propeller will suck in any loose line. It is important to get the lines wrapped up as far as possible before letting a boat too close; if possible signal or shout at them to approach you from upwind with the engine stopped.

'I need help' The international rescue signal

# The Self-Rescue Procedure

It has all gone pear shaped - both you and the kite are in the water and your only option is to pack up and paddle home. Your first priority is to make sure things do not get any worse. To minimise getting drifted any further downwind than necessary, be prepared to give up earlier rather than later.

Once the decision is made, you need to ensure the kite will not re-launch. This is done by making one tip line shorter than the other so that the kite sits with one tip into the wind.

If you have not already done so, activate the quick-release mechanism. Once on the end of the safety leash, you need to haul yourself back to the bar. To do this without getting line burned or tangled up, you should work your way up one line, taking car not to wrap it around your hand (in fact in lighter winds you can do this 'open handed') and pay the excess line well out to one side of you.

**1** Once with the bar, wind one of the steering (rear) lines on to the bar (end to end in figure eight as usual) until you have at least 2 metres (3 metres with a big kite) wound on.

**2** Lock this off securely with a hitch around the end of the bar. This stops the kite re-launching even if you drop the bar. (Note: your safety leash is still connected at this stage).

**3** Wind all the lines onto the bar as usual (only one will be under tension) until you are so close to the kite the tips are being pulled together slightly. Lock off all the lines securely with a hitch as before. You can now grab the kite by a tip (many models have handles to help you).

**4** If you are keeping the kite inflated, you can wrap the lines from the other tip of the kite around your harness hook; this allows you to bend it into a tight arc.

**5** You now have a choice: you can use the kite as a sail and drift in, if you are upwind of a safe landing area; or you can lie on the inflated kite and paddle in, or you can pack it up and swim, or you can sit on it. Use it as a float if you are sure rescue is on its way.

**6** Assuming you are on your own and do need to swim, you now need to deflate the main spar of the kite, or if it is a ram-air kite, open the dump valve. Most tube kites will have an oversize dump valve located either on the tip or at the centre. The tip is easier to use as you can roll the kite up toward it. Ram-air kites usually have a dump valve on each tip.

Open the valve and roll up the kite, leaving any rib spars inflated - they add buoyancy.

Don't forget to put the valve bung back in!

It is possible that you have a ram-air kite and it has been filled with a lot of water. If it is heavy and cannot be drained easily, you have no choice but to abandon it.

**7** Load the rolled kite onto your board, together with the bar, and start paddling!

It may be easier to lie on the top of the board and kite or possibly to pull it with the leash.

Do not abandon the kite and/or board unless there is obvious danger to you if you do not.

This procedure is very important, and should be taught early in your training programme.
(It is part of the BKSA level 2 syllabus)
It is in your interest to make sure you are familiar with what to do if things go wrong!

## Boat rescue

Pack up the kite in the same way while you await rescue. Be careful to wind up all the lines.

If the boat driver is not familiar with kites, make sure he approaches from upwind so that no lines/fabric can foul the propeller.

It is important that you always know where you are. If you are riding in an unfamiliar area, do not venture too far - it is easy to lose sight of landmarks if you are low in the sea with a swell.

Always ride within your abilities and with others, and if you do ride out at sea you may consider investing in some rocket flares. They are no bigger than a pack of cigarettes and can be stowed in a pocket of your harness.

If it all goes pear shaped and you do cut away from your kite or abandon your board, it is very important (and a legal requirement in the UK) that you inform the coastguard of what has happened.

In North East England in January 2002, kitesurf equipment was spotted drifting by a fisherman. The ensuing air-sea rescue effort involved a lifeboat and two helicopters and cost over £38,000.

The rider had just left his kit and gone home. This sort of thing does not endear us to the rescue services!

## Medical emergencies

Most of the above assumes that you are the casualty and that you are in reasonable shape. But of course this might not be the case. If it is you that is helping someone else, it is useful to know what the likely hazards are. There are a few useful bits of information that can help you.

The biggest hazards to kitesurfers are the potential for getting a lungful of water and drowning, and suffering from either hypothermia or dehydration.

These are pictures of an actual rescue at Safaga Egypt. The wind dropped quickly, leaving kites ditched and the riders facing a long swim back if Mohamamed and his Rib had not been handy!

## Drowning

If a fellow rider gets stunned or manages to get water in his lungs, the first priority is to clear his airway. This usually means getting his face out of the water, but it can also mean tilting his chin back if he has lost consciousness, as the airway could be blocked by the tongue. The second priority is to call for help if possible, or better still, send someone else to do so.

If he is not breathing, the third priority is to get some air into his system (don't bother trying to get the water out first). This is best done with mouth to mouth resuscitation. This is obviously very difficult to do in a swell with him draped half-way across a sinky little board. But if his heart is still beating, it is well worth a try, as one or two breaths might just jump-start the breathing reflex.

CPR (heart massage) is not practical in these circumstances, and research shows that a stopped heart has to be defibrillated within about 12 minutes to have any chance at all of restarting. If you are on the beach, his airway is clear and medical help has been called, the drill is to give 30 chest compressions, then 2 rescue breaths, and to keep repeating this pattern.

## Hypothermia

Hypothermia is a very real danger when sailing in colder water; good equipment is vital and knowing your own limits is the key to sailing safely.

Hypothermia is a drop in the body's core temperature, and wet skin combined with wind results in a very high wind chill factor, which is a very effective way to achieve it.

Being in cool water for prolonged periods is far more likely to kill you by hypothermia than by drowning.

Hypothermia comes on gradually, so learn to recognise the warning signs of shivering, pale skin, apathy, irrational behaviour, disorientation and sometimes belligerence.

The symptoms may not manifest themselves until the sailor is on the shore; stripping off a wetsuit in a windy car park can be the final straw.

Treatment is to get warm and dry, and give warm drinks and high-energy food like chocolate.

Do not allow the casualty any alcohol. Do not place the casualty close to a direct heart source.

If the casualty lies down or loses consciousness ensure that he is insulated from the ground.

Anyone who show signs of hypothermia should not be left alone and medical treatment should be sought.

To recap, anyone seen shivering and looking pale, or who seems belligerent, irrational or apathetic after kitesurfing should not be bought a drink. (That should save a few quid!)

## Sunburn

When on the water a high proportion of the sun's radiation is reflected upward from the surface, so the sailor is receiving a much higher dose of UV than if he were just lying on the beach.

Because the wind is cooling you by evaporating sweat and spray from your skin (the wind chill factor mentioned above), the heat of the sun is not as apparent, and the result is that it much easier to get burned.

This is unpleasant, and peeling feet and faces are not very attractive, but more importantly a good dose of sun can make you feel ill and spoil your sailing (and even your holiday), and sunburn is a major factor in the increasing incidence of skin cancer.

Too much sun is bad news. The only way to combat this is to cover up, wear a rash vest and a hat (unless you are very confident, this will need a cord under your chin!).

Sunglasses are also useful, but again they need a cord or 'croakie' so you do not lose them.

Any skin left exposed should be liberally slathered with high factor waterproof sun cream (with the notable exception of the soles of the feet!).

If you have been burned and have red skin, regular sun cream will not prevent more damage the next day; the only option is to cover up or use total sun block.

Note: lips are notoriously prone to wind & sunburn and the protection soon wears off, so use a separate chap stick and re-apply often.

## Dehydration

It may seem a bit strange being concerned by dehydration when doing a watersport,

but however wet you are you can still suffer from lack of water on the inside!

As a kitesurfer may be very active, out for long periods, sweating profusely and probably also wearing a wetsuit with no handy pockets for a water bottle, this is not uncommon.

Thirst, headaches, and possibly dizziness are the early symptoms. But by the time you feel dry-mouthed you are already suffering from serious dehydration. You should drink before you are thirsty.

For most sailors this means topping up on water (not sugary drinks, tea & coffee or beer!) before you venture out for a session.

Note: some recreational drugs, particularly Ecstasy, can cause profuse sweating and accelerate the onset of serious dehydration.

Take a bottle of water to the beach with you and keep topping up whenever you come ashore. If you are fresh off the aeroplane and sailing in a hotter climate than usual this is doubly important.

## Heat exhaustion

Heat exhaustion is the next stage if dehydration or sunburn is not treated, or if the casualty is already suffering from fluid loss through recent sickness or diarrhoea.

The symptoms are like dehydration but with cramps, weakness, dizziness and confusion, a rapid pulse and 'panting' respiration.

The treatment is to get the casualty cooled down (lie in the sea) and to drink water and if possible some weak salt solution. Recovery can seem quick but it takes some time to recover fully and it is advisable to seek medical attention.

In severe cases, or if left untreated, this can develop into heat stroke, which is very dangerous and can lead to unconsciousness, this is recognisable by a 'bounding' pulse and red flushed skin; sweating stops. Heat stroke requires hospitalisation.

# The Points of Sailing, Vectors and the Apparent wind

The diagram below (the wind rose) represents a plan view of all the possible directions available with you at the centre. The exact courses will vary depending on the board and kite being used and other factors.

The force of the wind is naturally trying to push you directly downwind, but because you can vector this force (discussed below) you can actually ride on any course shown in the indicated area.

## The Points of Sailing

### No-go zone

If you try and turn too far upwind with the kite, it will simply stop when it reaches the edge of the window and the power will decrease. If the board is turned

upwind too far, it will also have too great an angle between the direction of travel and the force applied by the kite; it will slow down, come off the plane, and start to sink. The no-go zone is therefore an effective brake for you. Turn upwind and you will stop.

However, it is worth noting that the kite does not like being forced to the edge of the window, and in strong winds it is quite possible to ride but be unable to make the kite go the edge of the window, and if you turn the board too far upwind while the kite is still well powered, you will be pulled off!

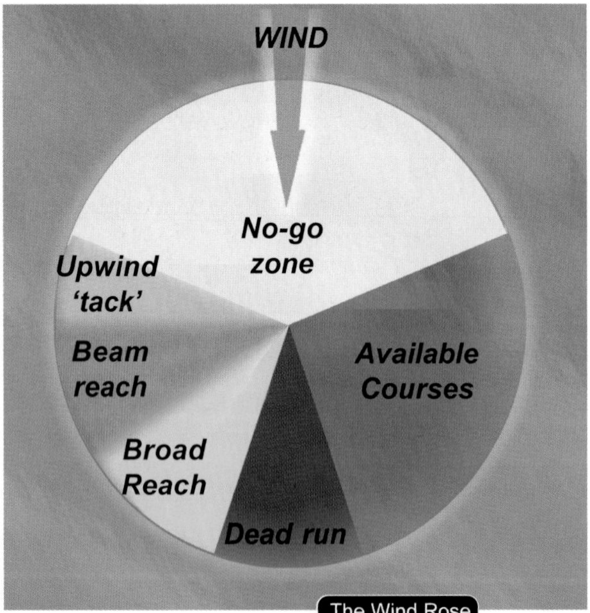

### Tacking

You can make progress upwind by tacking. The word 'tacking' is used in sailing to describe both the action of turning your craft by using its momentum to force the nose of the craft through the upwind no-go sector to change direction (not usually very practical on a kite powered craft).

It is also used to describe a course that is taking you upwind, and in this sense kitesurfers tack all the time. To ride to a point upwind of you, it is necessary to sail a course as far upwind as you can, and hold each beat (course) for as far as is practical (every turn will cost you some progress). And then, of course, make a neat, efficient turn and do the same the other way.

WIND

No-go zone

Upwind 'tack'

Beam reach

Available Courses

Broad Reach

Dead run

The Wind Rose

Some kites have wider windows than others and are better at upwind courses. Some boards are also more effective than others, so the exact angle you can achieve does vary considerably. All twin-tip boards also give the facility for making switch turns - quick changes of direction without much downwind drift - which can be critical in making progress upwind, especially if your beats are quite short.

It is because the no-go zone is so wide for kitesurfers that starting from a beach with a dead onshore wind can be tricky.

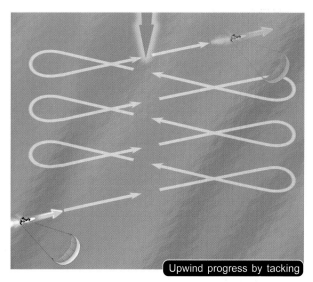
Upwind progress by tacking

### Beam reach

This simply means sailing a course roughly across the wind. A perfect beam reach is 90 degrees to the wind, but the term is used for any more or less crosswind beat.

Because holding a beam reach track or a slightly upwind track means you are burning up a lot of your available power on drag, by edging the board, and to a lesser extent losing some power by keeping the kite near the edge of the window, this course is a lot slower than a broad reach in the same wind conditions. Kitesurfers are much slower than windsurfers in this situation.

### Broad reach

This is the fastest point of sailing for kitesurfers; the board can be kept reasonably flat, minimising drag, and the kite can be worked through most of the power zone. On a broad reach a kitesurfer is pretty well the fastest thing (without an engine) on the water! Many riders will gradually work their way upwind for a few tacks, then turn onto a broad reach for a high-speed blast or two back to their start point.

### Dead run

This is de-power zone; if you try and head dead downwind, the board tends to catch up with the kite, so the power is lost and the board comes off the plane and wallows. The only way to prevent this is by adding some drag, and as soon as you turn the board to present an edge, the whole system powers up again and you are off on a broad reach.

It is perhaps possible to sink the tail of the board or progress in a series of short jumping turns, like a skier getting down a steep gully, but you can travel in the desired direction much better and faster with a few beats on a broad reach.

If you are generating plenty of drag by not being on the board at all, the de-power zone pretty much equates to your window for passive body-dragging! (i.e. without using a hand dragged to one side for steering.)

## Vectors

When a force acting in one direction such as the wind, is deflected or harnessed to generate a force in different direction, it is known as vectoring. The kite itself vectors the wind using its airfoil to fly forward, and the board vectors the force transmitted through the rider's feet to travel crosswind or upwind.

Remember the bicycle analogy. Ride the bike over a cliff and the force (gravity in this case) will act directly on you! Roll down a slope and the same force pulling the same way now provides a forward motion, the hill has vectored the force. Steer at an angle across the slope and it can be vectored even more, until eventually you will be going at close to 90 degrees to the original force and it will stop.

Unfortunately no-one has managed the trick of vectoring gravity so far that you can travel upwards, but that is exactly what kitesurfing does with our primary force, the wind. Damned clever, eh?

## Apparent wind

When you are riding at some speed, you will start to notice that the kite seems to be moving back away from the edge of the window and your course is curving downwind.

To prevent this you edge the board harder, which slows you down a bit and the kite flies forwards again, but as you speed up, back it goes! What you are experiencing is the phenomenon we call 'apparent' wind.

Wind is the name we give to moving air masses, but it feels the same and behaves the same way if it you that is actually doing the moving.

Imagine you are in a speed boat doing 20 knots (roughly 22mph) on a still day.

The 'wind' will be 20 knots in your face; if you launched a kite it would fly behind you.

On the same boat travelling at the same speed but at 90 degrees to a 'real' 20- knot

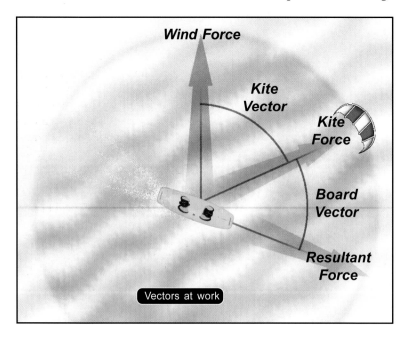

**Wind Force**

**Kite Vector**

**Kite Force**

**Board Vector**

**Resultant Force**

Vectors at work

wind, the apparent wind would be from midway between the true wind and the speed-through-the-air of the boat; the kite now would fly at an angle behind you.

This is exactly the situation when riding a kiteboard at speed - as your board moves faster, the apparent wind is coming from more ahead of you and the window moves back, taking the kite with it. Slow the board down by edging hard and creating drag and the window moves forward again. Interestingly, as your board speed increases and the apparent wind phenomenon occurs, you are not only changing the wind's direction, but you are also effectively increasing the wind speed, so the kite generates more power. It therefore becomes harder and harder work to edge the board at high speeds and keep an upwind course.

One way to help manage this situation is to ride with an activated de-power system to keep the kite flying fast and low near the edge of the window. When you do loft the kite and/or release the tension in the de-power loop, there is a big release of energy.

Good riders use this phenomenon to generate masses of stored energy in a radically edged board at high speed and then explosively release this power to make massive jumps.

# Dealing with Light Winds, High Winds and Waves

By now you may have already discovered that the wind is never perfect (except on the days you have missed, naturally). Apart from the direction, it is almost always either too light or too strong (or sometimes both on the same day). However, the range of winds that you can use, given the right techniques and equipment, is surprising.

## Light winds

If the wind is light when you arrive at the beach, and seems set to stay that way, your first weapon is to select the largest or most powerful kite available. Longer lines will take advantage of the wind gradient and give the kite the most power.

Check the surface of the water and the surrounding terrain; it may be that just one spot is the best, or that the wind is stronger further out from the beach. If it really is too calm, sometimes there is simply no option but to wait.

The start can be quite tricky if there is little power. The kite seems to be OK when you are standing on a solid surface, but as soon as you put your second foot in the board strap you will start drifting, therefore effectively reducing the wind strength. It is quite common for riders to get their feet sorted before they begin to work the kite for power, and in the few seconds of drifting they lose control authority and the kite stalls. In shallow water you can quickly stand down again and step back as you work the kite; if you are in deep water you are likely to lose it and you will have to forget the

If you need an anchor man to keep you down, it might be too strong!

Light breeze: Warm sea, BIG kite! *(Photo: Tracy Kraft, Cabrinha)*

board and keep the kite aloft by working it hard. This may mean body-dragging back to the beach.

If you have practiced beach starts, this is a great time to use them, as the drifting problem can be eliminated. Do remember to point a little more downwind than usual and crouch low on the board (especially as the kite turns), as this helps your balance when the pull is weakest. If you have a choice of board, choose the largest; a small wakeboard or similar can be a major handicap in light winds.

While you are sailing you can maximise power in a couple of ways. You can choose a more downwind track, or increase airspeed of the kite by working it in an aggressive pattern. If it is very marginal, you may have to do both. Crouching to lower your centre of gravity closer to the

board helps you stay upright in an underpowered situation. Try not to let the kite get too low as you dive it hard for power - there will be slightly less wind lower down, as mentioned above, and as the control will be sluggish too, it is very easy to catch a wave with the kite and ditch it (a favourite trick !). A large ditched kite on a very light day can be very difficult or impossible to re-launch.

Of course you may simply not have enough wind to ride fast enough for the board to support your weight. If this occurs, you have no option but to body-drag back to shore. For this reason very light winds are quite dangerous if the breeze is offshore, as even a rider who is confident about making upwind progress can come unstuck if the wind drops. So it is important that you remain aware of the changing conditions and have a good idea of the forecast for the day. Do not be tempted by the prospect of stronger winds farther out from shore to venture long way out to sea in marginal conditions.

## Strong winds

The opposites apply! If you are still on the beach, choose a smaller kite; you can also 'set' most de-power systems by shortening the front lines for max speed. If the kite is still overwhelming you and there is not a safe beach downwind, you may have to admit defeat and wait for the wind to drop (see below).

Never launch a kite in a very strong wind if the area downwind is at all hazardous. The commonest cause of serious accidents is the rider being dragged into rocks, roads, jetties or other obstacles.

If you are riding and the wind picks up, you can make use of your de-power loop to handle the increased force. If you are already using this or if you have a 2-line kite, you can better manage the power

by taking the kite to the edge of the window.

Lofting it to the top of the window will also work, but this does mean that you will inevitably drift downwind. Once going downwind it is very hard to get the kite back down and to the side and regain directional control. The best plan is to try and control the power by brute force! Edge the board very hard and thereby create massive drag; this should give you the authority (if you have the muscles!) to allow you get the kite to fly to the forward edge of the window and get you moving upwind. The more upwind the track, the easier it is to control the power. Try and keep the kite really low as this will also minimise the power and help you edge the board.

Gybing, particularly on a kite without a de-power system can be a real problem in this situation. If you do lose it you will end up following the kite downwind. This is fine if there is a friendly beach in that direction - if not, you may have to dump the kite and may be in for a long drag while you reel it in and pack it up, followed by a long paddle!

Strong winds are no problem as long as the size of your kite matches the conditions.

A smaller board may also help you stay in control more easily.

### A note of caution:

A dropped kite may keep re-launching itself in strong winds and will keep dragging you downwind. It is essen-

tial that you have a properly functioning release system that completely kills the kite, and that you know how to use it. If you expect to be riding in strong conditions, having a cutaway system or carrying a hook knife to escape completely if you get into real trouble is a wise investment.

Do not forget you are responsible for others as well as yourself, riding in nuclear conditions may be a risk you are prepared to take, but if there are other water users around (and windsurfers love this kind of weather), make sure you give them a wide berth. A 2mm diameter line travelling at 30 knots with you on one end of it is a lethal weapon!

The most hazardous part of riding in strong conditions is coming in to the beach. If you can get a helper to catch the kite while you are still in the water, this is the best solution.

An inflated kite on a windy beach will just keep blowing away, thrashing itself to bits and causing a hazard to others. Your only option is to dump your kite (preferably in the water) on the emergency leash, wind in a few metres of one steering line, lock that off on the bar, and wind in the rest of the lines. (See the self rescue procedure in Chapter 16).

Kites fitted with a 5th line are much easier to handle in this situation.

## Waves

Many people (particularly outside the UK) learn to kitesurf on the flat water of a lake or reservoir, or in a sheltered bay or lagoon. But if you learn in Britain, or as you progress to blasting in stronger winds or buy your own kit and head for the local beach, you will soon start to encounter waves.

The mix of strong winds and open water always produces some small waves, and dealing with this chop is simply a matter of keeping the board slightly more nose up and flexing your knees. When you ride in deeper water, or on the coast of a

Deep water swell

In force 4-5 winds the swell breaks, white horses start to appear.

The wave encounters the bottom and is pushed up into a shore break

larger sea or ocean, the waves start to change character.

The surface of the water has had time to react to pushing of the wind over a long distance to form a swell - the typical heaving surface of the sea.

The height of the swell depends on the wind strength and the 'fetch' – the distance the uninterrupted wind has had to develop the swell.

A storm hundreds of miles away can start this process and the bigger the ocean the bigger the potential for swell. If the swell grows too high (more than one seventh the distance between the peaks), it will start to break and form whitecaps. This starts to happen when the wind reaches force 4, or 15 -18 mph.

The real fun starts when the swell approaches the land and is resolved into a line of breakers.

If it is coming straight at the shore and the sea bed is the right angle the waves can grow to massive proportions. In shallower approaches or with the shore line at an angle to the swell, the waves can lose much of their energy and height before they arrive.

With a little local knowledge and experience and knowing the tides for their local spot, riders soon become expert at forecasting the likely height and power of the waves. More information on tides is given in Chapter 5.

Starting in a shore break needs a good technique as the board is shoved around by each wave. Strong waves and a cross-onshore wind can make it very difficult to get deep enough to start without grounding the fins. A helper hanging on to your harness can be useful while you get your feet in and choose your moment.

White water or surf is a mixture of air bubbles and water and is less 'solid' than blue water. The board will need quite a lot more speed to get going and support your weight in these conditions. Light winds and starting in surf are a very difficult combination for this reason, as you need to be well powered up to get going and to climb the waves.

A directional board is much better at upwind progress, has higher volume and the rocker (curved up nose) together with a bigger fin this makes it far easier to manage in wave conditions.

If you plan to spend much time wave riding then a directional board is a very useful bit of kit.

Landing on the beach is also more hazardous; it is very easy to lose your board in a strong shore-break and more than one rider has run into problems trying to deal with an escaping board and landing a kite in a strong wind.

Directional boards have a noticeable advantage in waves

The key is to time your landing by following in the back of a wave, then smartly step off the board, scoop it up, and make the beach before the next one gets you. A helper to catch the kite in this situation is very useful, and vital if the landing area is very restricted.

Keep riding waves long enough and you will inevitably get knocked off your board and have it surf away from you. This is why surfers use a board leash and a few kitesurfers choose do the same.

A leashed board is also much more likely to hit you and you are more likely to hit the water or the bottom hard in any case in wave conditions, so a helmet is a crucial piece of gear for wave riding.

Sailing in waves is both the most technical and most challenging aspect of the sport; keeping good control on a constantly changing surface is full of surprises and demands the mastery of new skills. A good session in wave conditions is about the most fun you can have on a kiteboard!

# Getting Air: Jumping

One of the most appealing aspects of kitesurfing is the potential for awesome jumps.

Windsurfers and water-skiers can make jumps by speeding over a ramp - usually in the form of waves or the wake of a boat, but a kitesurfer can use the lift of the wing to gain serious altitude even when the surface is flat. The potential for getting airborne is what makes kitesurfing so different - and such an exiting sport to take part in and watch. It is a truly three-dimensional sport.

## How do you initiate a jump?

- First you need plenty of energy, so get the board travelling as fast as you can, holding an edge, with the de-power activated. Simply switch the kite direction, sending it up towards the top and rear of the window.

- Bend your knees and keep edging the board hard as you feel the power surge upwards (as the kite nears the top of the window).

- Release the board edge and jump by straightening your legs. If you have enough power and lift, the board should clear the water. You are better off if you hit the water again moving, so bring the kite back down into the front of the window again.

Note: Do not attempt to jump when using a board leash.

While airborne it is much easier to control the board and pivot it into a good landing position if you bend your knees again to bring it closer to your body.

Of course there is no edge to stop you, and with the kite moving downwind while you are airborne, a small hop will not have much effect, but this means that on a larger jump you will be drifting downwind. To cope with the landing, you will need to angle the board slightly downwind as well, so that it is in line with your direction of travel. Once down safely, you can dive the kite and edge the

board to recover your upwind line. The board will need to land reasonably flat - if you hook a wave or dig in the front of the board end then it's water up the nose time (again)!.

Top tip: let go of the bar with your rear hand when airborne, this automatically accelerates the kite forward into position for landing.

A jump will, of course, mean a significant drift downwind from your original track, so after each one check you are still able to ride safely back to the beach! Jumping over people or objects is dangerous, and you can lose your board whilst airborne. NEVER try and jump

over windsurfers, swimmers or any other person, and always make sure you have plenty of space downwind - landing on water is fine, but landing on a beach is likely to be painful. Always allow at least three line lengths of clear water downwind of your expected landing point (more in strong winds). It is possible that you will hit a gust or a thermal and get hoisted higher or for longer than you were expecting.

Jumping is not without potential hazards!

Hopefully you are attached to the board by your footstraps - it is important that the feet are jammed well in, as losing one strap can mean a nasty twist to the remaining leg when you land again. If you have lost a foot it is advisable to kick out the other foot as well before you hit the water, to minimise any risk. A big directional board will be hard to control

as it is heavy, easily caught by the wind and your feet will be close together and well behind the board's centre of gravity. Bending your knees and bringing it close to your body will help with control, but it can take considerable muscle power to keep it flat and pointing the right way. For this reason jumps are much easier to perform on smaller lighter twin tips, where the feet are more symmetrically placed on the board. Riders who like to get big air jumps use the smallest boards they can.

If you do lose the board during a jump or landing you want to be able to kick it away, so using a leash is a very bad idea when jumping. The last thing you want is a board being catapulted at your head as you wipe out! Wear a helmet.

Avoid letting go of the bar completely when you are jumping. You may see pictures in the magazines of this, but the riders have no kite control at this point and letting go of a bar is a lot easier than getting it back with both hands in a hurry.

Jumping is just the start - you can do twists, loops and board off tricks. It is possible to execute multiple 360s, railies (where the board is grabbed with one hand) and a whole range of tricks. Top-class wakeboarders already perform phenomenal stunts, and with the additional lift and airtime afforded by a kite, inverted (head down) tricks, handle-passes - where the bar is passed around the body (you need a modified leash attachment for this)

To make a change in midair, the jump must be of sufficient duration for you to be able to take it across the window and dive it into the window the other way before touchdown.

Heel-to-toe changes need very little time or height, so you can do this switch on a short chop-hop while still moving quite fast. This move is the perfect setup for a fast carving turn back from toe-to-heel. Nice!

Rider: Dimitri Maramenides Photographer: Bill Mielcke

and the combination of several free-style tricks into a flowing routine. There is huge scope for improvisation; the sport is young and there is plenty of potential for you invent your own moves.

You can use the jump as a platform for making a direction change (an aerial gybe or transition) or to switch from heel-side to toe-side riding.

Invert

Board Rider: Tom Hebert Photographer: John Carter

When you jump, you are very likely to be hooked into your de-power system. If this is the case, you must be aware that hanging from the de-power loop will dive the kite to some extent as you are airborne. This is actually ideal if there is plenty of lift, but do ensure you remain aware of what the kite is doing as you are airborne. One common problem with early jumps is that the kite is moving upward as you leave the water and it 'overflies' you (i.e. gets past the top edge of the window), the angle of attack of the airfoil get too low and the kite 'luffs', i.e. starts a fluttering dive and hits the water shortly after you do! To avoid this, start diving the kite forward a little earlier.

When you are doing big jumps with time to play while you are airborne, you can go for an aerial kite loop; this needs considerable space on most inflatable models, but as the kite dives while you are climbing, can result in the rider getting higher than the kite.

The handle pass is a trick that has evolved from wakeboarding competition and involves passing the kite bar around behind your back, allowing you to rotate in midair. The problem here is that the rider gets twisted up in the leash. (Wakeboarders, of course, do not have any leash.) To combat this, some harnesses incorporate a sliding connection (usually clips on a curved bar around the riders back) that allows the leash to pass from one side of the harness to the other. These connections are affectionately known as suicide leashes.

Jumps and airborne tricks and are the basis of much freestyle competition. It is this three-dimensional potential that makes kitesurfing such a different and spectacular sport.

# Understanding the Weather

As with most outdoor activities, we first need to decide what the weather is going to be like so that we can choose our venue (or choose to stay at home).

## Weather forecasts

Step one is simply looking out of the window, but the problem here is that you can only see what it is like now. What you need is to know how the weather will develop during the next few hours, and for that you need a forecast.

TV is very good on general weather - if it will be sunny or if it will be windy for example. From this you can gain a good idea of whether conditions are worth checking out further. The better TV forecasts feature a synoptic chart with isobars (lines joining points of equal pressure) and frontal systems (see fig 20.1).

This type of chart is also available from the met office as a fax, or on the internet.

The simple rule when checking out a synoptic chart is that the closer together the isobars, the stronger the wind will be. The wind strength and direction will be shown at various points on a chart but, inevitably, not just where you want! To know the direction at a given spot, you do need to be able to 'read' the chart yourself.

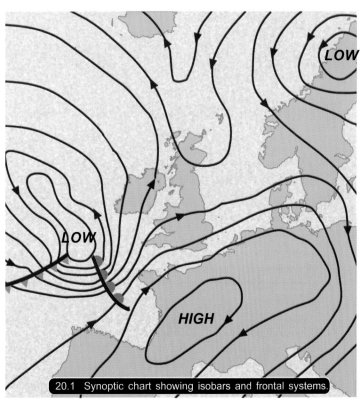

20.1 Synoptic chart showing isobars and frontal systems.

Useful forecasts can also be gained from the radio; the best of these in the UK is undoubtedly the Radio 4 shipping forecast (broadcast daily at 17:50hrs). This gives actual readings from coastal stations and sea areas.

Of course, you do need to know where the sea areas are. (See below)

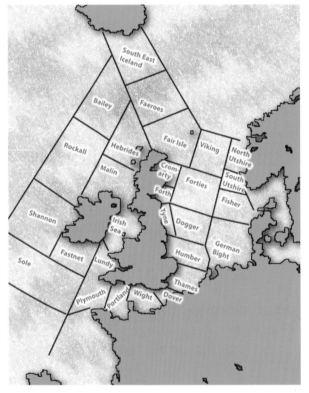

Finally, there are a number of telephone forecasts available; these vary considerably between, 'It will be a nice day', and good accurate wind and weather data. In the UK almost all get their information from the met office and you can get a list of what forecasts are available. Forecast details and many useful websites are listed in the 'information' section.

Some sailing, windsurfing and other sports clubs now have their own automated weather stations that you can access by phone. These give you the exact conditions now and the trend over the last hour or two. The 'wendy windblows ' coastal stations are especially useful as they are located at favourite windsurfing and kitesurfing spots and they also give tide states.

Details of one such system can be found at www.wendywindblows.com

## Basic meteorology

The weather is a huge and complex subject, but a grasp of the basic mechanics of a weather system will help you plan your venue more accurately and give you a good idea of what to expect next. Here is the quick guide to the main features:

### Depressions and Fronts

Depressions are areas of relatively low atmospheric pressure. Air can rise easily in these regions and as a result depressions are frequently associated with cloud and rain. Depressions often form where air masses of different temperatures meet. The division between these air masses is known as a front. Because the air masses on either side of the front have different characteristics, these fronts become irregular and develop 'waves' along their length. The actual process is largely triggered by the high altitude jet stream winds.

A wave on the front is the first sign of a depression being created.

As the depression develops, the pressure drops, and the winds increase. The air masses are now arranged in sectors, and are typically divided by a warm front followed by a cold front (shown on the diagram)

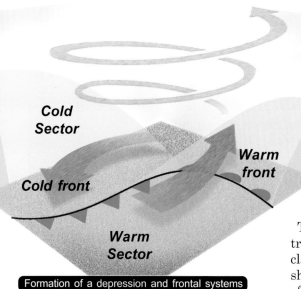

Cold
Sector

Warm
front

Cold front

Warm
Sector

Formation of a depression and frontal systems

Wind will flow anti-clockwise around a low pressure area. If you look at the synoptic chart above you will see that the wind direction at the surface is actually biased slightly inward toward the centre of the Low - rather like water flowing down a plug hole. (These directions are only true for the Northern Hemisphere - in the Southern Hemisphere the flow is in the opposite direction).

The majority of the 'weather' is concentrated around the frontal zones, and to clarify the characteristics fig 20.2 below shows a cross-section through each type of front.

As the depression gradually fills and weakens over the course of a few days, the cold front gradually overtakes the warm front and the result is an occluded front. Occlusions can be just like having one front turning into the next, giving miserable conditions for many hours, but quite often they occur quite late in the life of a depression and are fairly weak and are marked by nothing more than a thickening band of cloud for an hour or two, or a few spots of rain.

A warm front is simply the approaching warm light air sliding up over the denser cool air. It will first appear as high cirrus cloud a few hours before the front itself. This cloud gradually lowers and thickens into nimbo-stratus or strato-cumulus; these are rain clouds, and light rain will fall, growing heavier as the cloud base drops. The wind 'backs' - that is, swings anti-clockwise, and strengthens. As the front passes over, the rain slackens, the cloud base rises again and the wind 'veers' (swings clockwise, for example from south to west). Though you may

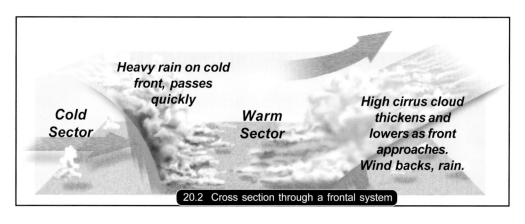

Heavy rain on cold
front, passes
quickly

Cold
Sector

Warm
Sector

High cirrus cloud
thickens and
lowers as front
approaches.
Wind backs, rain.

20.2 Cross section through a frontal system

not notice it, you will now be in a warm sector with higher air temperatures. The passage of a warm front from the first sight of high cloud can take many hours, so once the rain starts you can expect it to last a while.

A cold front is similar in that it 'shovels' warm moist air upward ahead of it but looks quite different to the ground observer. The first signs are heavy rain, and possibly thunder, with cumulonimbus clouds on an active front. There may be a 'gust front' if the clouds are very large. This is an area of strong wind, which may extend some way in front of the clouds - this type of sudden wind can be very dangerous. As the front arrives, the wind increases and veers. After the passage of a cold front the cloud lifts quickly and the colder air may give a noticeable drop in temperature. Often, if the air is cold and the sun is shining, this may lead to thermal activity inland soon afterwards with gusty winds.

Cold fronts can be more violent than warm fronts, because they travel faster and the warm air is pushed up more quickly. The whole front may arrive and be gone in a couple of hours, so if it is chucking it down due to a cold front when you arrive it may well be worth waiting.

### High pressure systems

High pressure regions, or anti-cyclones, can be visualised as huge mounds of air, the additional weight of which is constantly sinking and flowing downwards and outwards and which acts as a lid that prevents thermals climbing to form cumulus clouds.

A frontal system moving in

The weather in the summer is often hot and may be humid with little wind. When a strong high is established directly overhead it may last many days, and unless a sea breeze occurs (see below) the kitesurfing possibilities may be very limited, as the winds will be very light. However, if the high is off to one side of your region, it can result in a steep pressure gradient, when the opposite is true: the air is accelerated as it flows around the side of a high, and can give strong winds and clear skies.

In winter the trapped, warmer, more humid air can be cooled at night by contact with the cold ground and fog or mist is common on high pressure days.

### Micrometeorology

Once we have the basic picture from the forecast, we must add some local detail; this is best predicted by being aware of the characteristics of the wind. It will tend to split around a headland, for example, but will be 'pulled in' to a bay with high ground around it.

When the wind is cross shore on any coast that is not straight, there will be areas of wind shadow behind promontories or any large obstacle, like a harbour wall.

In places where the wind crosses land before a stretch of water the airflow will be affected by the factors affecting that land, such as thermals. A thermal is a bubble of air that is heated by a warm surface (like a town or a south facing slope). As the warm air expands and rises, nearby air rushes in to replace it, and the result is felt by the sailor as firstly a lull and then a gust of wind. Piled-up white cumulus clouds often mark thermals. The bigger and taller the clouds, the stronger the thermals. When conditions are good for this kind of convection the air is referred to by weathermen as unstable - and that is just how it feels.

Because air is affected by drag, and land is much rougher and therefore 'draggier' than the sea, the wind a few hundred metres offshore is very often stronger than close in. So if the wind is close to your limit for a specific kite size on the beach, it is likely to be more powerful a bit further out.

Sailors tend to look ahead, but it is worth looking over your leading shoulder to check what is upwind of you. Gusts and stronger winds are marked by ruffled patches on the surface which always look darker, so you can anticipate approaching patches of wind (or lulls). The water surface is a good indicator of strength and consistency of the wind.

Even if it does not feel too strong where you are rigging, white caps or streaks or foam are a powerful indicator that it is blowing up out there.

### Sea breezes

These are an important feature of coastal weather. A sea breeze is formed when there is a light prevailing wind or none at all, and the general heating of the land creates a lot of convection as the arm air rises. The cooler air lying on the water then flows in to the low pressure area inland, and the breeze gradually swings more onshore and strengthens as the day progresses. In the evening, as the land cools more quickly than the sea, this process is reversed, so at dusk a sea breeze

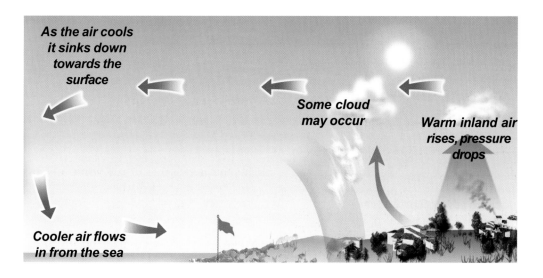

**As the air cools it sinks down towards the surface**

**Some cloud may occur**

**Warm inland air rises, pressure drops**

**Cooler air flows in from the sea**

may die away quickly and as night falls a land breeze may develop (well worth knowing if you are sailing well out from shore on a sea-breeze day and its getting late...).

In many countries with warm climates this is a daily phenomenon, and the sea breezes are a standard feature of many well-known coastal kitesurfing venues. Even around the UK coast it can be as much as Force 3 and above on hot summer days, making apparently windless days quite usable to those in the right place.

A light onshore breeze can be reinforced by the sea breeze as well, making a day that seems a little too gentle inland actually quite strong at the beach.

In many regions this daily thermal cycle and wind phenomenon is so regular that it is known by a specific name, such as 'Meltemi' in parts of Greece.

### Wind gradient.

A further characteristic of the wind worth consideration is the fact that it gets stronger the higher it is from the surface. This is because the drag of the air mass on the water or land slows it down at the surface, but as there is less drag higher up the wind speed is almost always greater. To kitesurfers this is relevant because a higher kite (on longer lines for example) will be in a stronger airflow and generate more power than one close to the surface. This is also of interest to us if we are lucky enough to have a choice of sailing ven-

ues, as a lake or reservoir at, say, 700ft. above sea level, will enjoy a stronger wind than the coast on the same day. (Unless it is sea-breeze of course!)

Useful weather forecasts and websites are listed in the information section.

# Packing, Transporting and Caring for Your Equipment

## General care of your gear

When you have finished surfing for the day it is pretty likely that your gear will be wet, sandy or both. Packing up a kite and lines when they are wet, and then storing them for some time can cause quite a few problems.

Any sand trapped inside the kite cells or simply wrapped up in the fabric can be very abrasive. It is well worth trying to fly the kite dry and then shaking off any loose sand before packing on a clean surface such as grass. Of course this is not always possible, so the next best thing is to remove as much of the sand as you can by rinsing the kite (in fresh water if available) at the earliest opportunity.

The same applies to your harness and wetsuit, so a 20-minute washing session when you get home is generally a good idea! If you have been riding on the sea, the salt in the water will crystallise inside the cells of foil kites when they dry out; the crystals, whilst not as bad as sand, can also abrade the fabric and weaken the lines by crystallising inside the sheath in among the fibres.

Again, the best way to mini-

There's often more than one way to get to the beach!

Rinsing off with fresh water

Walking along the beach: note the kite is safely over the water

Half deflated kite

mise this problem is rinsing with fresh water. Many schools or kite centres will keep a tub of fresh water handy for the purpose.

Apart from the problems of wear, old water (from the sea or a lake), when left for a few days or weeks, tends to smell pretty bad, so keeping your kite and wetsuit clean will also help the atmosphere in your house or car as well!

### Kite care

Inflatable spar kites are single skinned, so they suffer much less from sand damage, but the results of being dragged over sharp rocks or other hazards can be quite serious, as it is possible to puncture one of the inflatable tubes.

Carrying an inflated kite is best done with the kite inverted and the centre of the leading edge spar tucked under your arm.

Drying kites is most effectively done by flying them, but if you are going to lay them out on grass or hang them up somewhere, make sure they are out of direct sunlight, or that they are packed up as soon as they are dry.

Carrying an inflatable kite
(Photo: Tracy Kraft)

The nylon or polyester fabrics that are commonly used in kite construction will only stand a few hundred hours of direct exposure to UV (depending on their weight and the colour) before they start to lose their impermeability and structural strength. This gradual deterioration is most apparent when the colours start to fade. The brightest colours, such as pink and yellow, will be the first to go, and fabrics in these colours can have as little as half the life expectancy of duller colours. This phenomenon is well known in the paragliding world, and is one of the reasons that kites from those manufacturers also making paragliders are rarely in fluorescent colours.

When you are not using your kite, pack it away or cover it up with something and it will last much longer.

Lines also benefit from being stored clean and dry, and although Dyneema (known as Spectra in the US) is a very strong, flexible and long-lived material, it does have a tendency to shrink when exposed to high temperatures. It is advisable not to leave kite lines uncovered in a car in direct sunlight, for example.

Packing a ram-air kite is best done opening the dump valve and squeezing the air out by laying it on its top surface; if one tip is pointed into the wind it will be much easier to manage. (If there

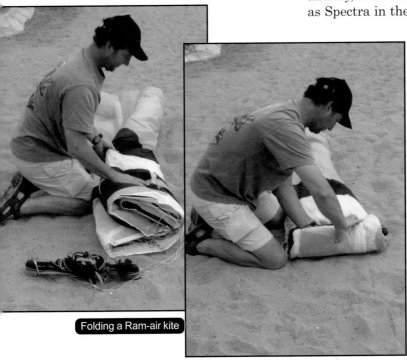
Folding a Ram-air kite

are two of you, helping each other makes this process much simpler) You can then either fold the tips to the centre (or if it is too windy, fold the kite a few panels at a time from the tip). Either way, make sure all the suspension lines remain on the top of the kite and get folded into the fabric - loose lines can easily get damaged in zips, etc). Once folded lengthwise, gently squeeze out the air, starting at the trailing edge. Valved kites may still need a bit of persuasion to deflate, but do not attempt to crush the air out too quickly as this will weaken the fabric and the seams (especially when wet). When the kite is deflated, fold it from the trailing edge to the size you need for you bag or rucksack, then secure it with a strap or by putting it in the bag.

If you have an inflatable spar kite you can deflate just the main leading edge spar and then loosely roll the rest into a long fat tube. This is, of course, very bulky, but is OK for short-term storage (though it does increase the risk of damage). Most kite bags now unzip to provide a full length storage space for a half-deflated kite.

To store it for long periods, or transport it safely, it will need to be fully deflated.

Note that ribs may go a little soft over time due to changes in air pressure or temperature. (In fact a kite ditched in cold water for a while can also lose quite a bit of its internal pressure.)

### Lines

The lines can either be wound onto your bar whilst still connected to the kite, or they can be removed completely. This is simply a matter of personal preference, though removing the lines from the kite will make it easier to lay them out without the risk of twisting. When the lines are being wound, the best technique is to use the figure 8 pattern. In this way each loop traps the preceding one. This prevents any loops falling off the bar out of order (a major cause of tangles). Many

Storing half-inflated kites

bars will feature some kind of shock-cord of Velcro locking strap at each end, or even a bar bag if you are lucky, to keep them secure in the kite bag.

### Boards

Boards are extremely tough in many ways, but they are also easy to scratch or damage by knocking them on a sharp object like a small rock, (or the corner of a car door!)

Always rinse off any sand sticking to your board, and if you are transporting it in a bag, try and let it dry before packing it up. (This is as much for the benefit of the bag as the board.) If the board is going inside a car, make sure it cannot flop around or has anything sharp near it. If it travels on the roof rack, get some padding around the rack bars. You can buy purpose-built pads from most water sports shops, or regular pipe lagging from a DIY store will also work perfectly.

It may seem obvious, but it is much better for the board to travel on the roof upside down so that the nose is curved down towards the screen and the fins are pointing upwards.

The fins (and your head) are less likely to get damaged like this as you get stuff out of the back of the car, and with many hatch-back or estate cars, the tailgate will swing up with quite a lot of force when it is opened and may hit the fins.

A padded board bag is a good idea to store and protect your gear, and is vital if you are travelling on a plane, train, etc, where your kit will be treated as baggage. If this is the case, it is obviously worth removing the fins completely and storing them in a separate bag. It also makes it much easier to carry everything, and if you need to walk a good distance from the car with your board, kite, wetsuit, towel, lunch, camera and deckchair it is invaluable!

## Dealing with damaged gear

### Boards

If you should be unlucky enough to damage your board, how you deal with it depends upon the material the board is con-

Ready for a major board repair

Professional repair (this is club Mistral, Safaga, Egypt)

structed from. While it is possible to re-pair some minor damage yourself, any-thing that fractures the outer casing of the board and reveals the foam core is going to need expert attention. A variety of different materials are used to con-struct boards and each need different techniques and materials to repair; the best advice is to take it to a windsurf or surf shop where an experienced member of staff can advise you.

In the case of small dry dents, the best advice is to use some 'ding stick' – this is available from all good dealers and con-sists of two tubes or sticks of epoxy putty that can be mixed together to give a quick-drying and hardwearing filler.

## Kites

If you have small rip in your kite fabric (less than about 2cm), this can gener-ally be repaired with ripstop tape. This can be found in a variety of colours at most kite dealers, windsurf shops or chandler's stores. Ripstop tape is self-adhesive and easy to apply, but do take care to round off any corners, which will prevent fraying and peeling away, and leave a good margin around the damage. It is important to lay the damaged area out flat and make sure it is clean and dry before applying a patch. A poor job will leave stress-marks in the fabric around the repair, making it both more obvious and less effective.

A single patch on the one side of the kite is OK for very small tears (up to 1cm), and these are practically invisible. Any-thing larger and you will need to place another patch on the outside as well. The two patches should be of different sizes so that there is no point where the edges match. This can cause a 'flex' point, which will be liable to damage.

If some gentle heat is applied to these patches (a cool iron, for example), the patch becomes very effectively welded to the fabric. Sticking patches on dusty or damp fabric, on the other hand, is a short-term fix.

Blown out internal ribs or significant tears of 5cm or more should be patched and sewn with a zigzag stitch to make a good repair. Ram-air kites may need to be partially dismantled along the trail-ing edge to be able to do this, and these are jobs best done by a professional.

Inflatable spar kites are very easy to maintain in one respect, as the kite is single surfaced and easy to patch. How-ever, a puncture in a spar can badly af-

Major blowout! Tube needs replacing...

Push in the valves

Tie lines to the bladder tips.

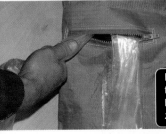

Release the other tip and pull out the bladder through the zipped opening

Remove bladder from kite leaving lines in place

Submerge the bladder to locate any leaks before patching or replacing. Always recheck a bladder a few hours after a repair before replacing in the kite

fect the performance and handling. Even a small puncture or leak in the main leading edge spar can render the kite unusable. The only course of action in these cases is to remove the inflatable tube from the fabric sleeve and repair it with either a drop of rubber solution glue or a patch. Glue can be used for tiny pin-prick type leaks; these will have to be located first, of course, and this is done by immersing the tube in water and checking for bubbles. Many inflatable spar kites are supplied with some small patches which are very effective. However, any damage greater than about 0.5cm means the tube is best discarded and replaced with a new one; the same is true of any tube with a faulty valve.

When you are removing the tubes from the kite, always remember to tie a piece of line to the narrow end first! (There are small velcro openings to enable you to get at the tubes to do this). Without a line to pull the repaired or replacement tube back into place, you will find it next to impossible to re-assemble your kite!

## Lines

A broken line when riding can be a serious problem and involve a long swim back to shore. It is therefore well worth getting into the habit of checking your lines regularly for weak spots or wear. The knots are particularly prone to damage, and are already the weakest spots on the line, so they deserve close attention. If a broken line is repaired at sea by knotting it, it must be replaced as soon as possible as it will inevitably soon break again. A single line break may be just bad luck, but if a line breaks more than once it is safer to simply replace them both. Most experienced riders will carry a spare set of lines.

Regular checks of your lines, leashes and chicken loop are critical.

Lines should be replaced every 100 hours of riding or every year, whichever is the sooner. (You can save the old set as emergency spares!)

## Harness and other components

The harness lines, chicken loop or strop that you hook into is also worth regular inspection - because of the constant movement and pressure on them, they do wear out surprisingly quickly and can cause you problems if they should snap.

Safety leashes must be regularly inspected and the quick release system operated periodically. The mechanisms can become stiff of jammed, especially after prolonged use in salty water.

# Buggies, Mountain boards & Snow kiting

For hundreds of years wind power was the main form of locomotion on water. Sailing ships were the premier form of long distance transport, and they become very sophisticated and efficient vessels. Wind power never really found a niche for land transport, primarily because the terrain was too rough. The few areas where it could have been used, such as snowfields or perhaps prairies, did not support much traffic and in any event horses, reindeer, or sled dogs were available and much more adaptable.

In recent times we have relied on engines, and it is really only a tiny group of people who have tried to use wind power for locomotion on land and they have only done so for recreation with land yachts. There are thousands of people who have sailed a yacht or dinghy on water for every one who has tried it on land! But kites are changing all that.

## Buggies

Traction kites are potentially more efficient than sails, and one of the first uses of traction kites was to power small three-wheel buggies. These machines have been around for quite a few years, and the interest in kitesurfing has stimulated many riders to try buggying too. Many of the skills are transferable, and buggies have the added advantage of being less dependent on a specific wind direction, and they allow you stay warm and dry(ish) in winter.

Learning to kite buggy is relatively easy, and because they have such low rolling resistance, they can be used with great success in winds that would be hopelessly light for kitesurfing.

A buggy typically costs around £300- 400 and is capable of 40mph plus on a smooth beach. They can be used on asphalt in the lightest of breezes and grass, soft sand, dirt and dunes can all be buggied, given the right combination of wheels and wind!

Photo: www.extremesportphotos.com

Photo: U-Turn

A 4-line open cell ram-air kite of some-where in the 2.5 to 6m range is the norm for buggying (or parakarting, as many prefer to term it). The precise control of these types allows relaunching of nosed-in kites without moving from your seat, and excellent power control. You will al-ready know that a typical water kite in sine wave mode has a powerful pull in the dive but a flat spot as you turn it back for the climb phase; parakarters can simply continue the dive into an inside turn (kite loop) to keep the kite's air speed high and deliver continuous power.

But the main reason for using a 4-line kite on handles is safety. The ground is a lot harder than water and may have obstacles like rocks, fences and people! The ability to stall the kite and kill the power by whacking both brakes on is vi-tal for safe operation in this environ-ment.

Getting up on two wheels, 360 spins and jumps are all regular tricks, and many parakarters take part in hotly contested races. These can be simple pursuit races around a course or complex cats cradle tasks requiring navigating obstacles,

Yeah, go for it dude!

Yeeee haaaa!

Photos: ww

Photo: www.extremesportphotos.com

tacking upwind and tactical skills.

The basic skill in using a buggy lies in controlling the tension between the kite and yourself - if you steer too much towards the kite you will start to overtake it, the lines will go slack and it will stall - turn too far upwind and you may find the kite is pulling you backwards out of the seat. Try this in a strong wind and you may find yourself having an 'out of buggy experience' – think of ejector seats and you will get the picture!

It is pretty simple to manage the basics of maintaining a course; most people with some kiting experience can be taught in an hour or two. Learning to gybe is next, and again this is pretty straightforward - loft your kite and kick the front wheel hard over to turn sharply, then bring the kite back down into the new front half of the window. Making good upwind progress and following a 'broad reach' downwind track requires more practice, but it is an addictive activity and every hour spent flying a kite improves your skills!

aaoooohhh...

photos.com

CARUUUUMPH!!!!!

Oooh, thank god I had that helmet on

Photo: www.extremesportphotos.com

cipally concerned with racing, and offers coaching and advice as well as organising race and fun meetings at venues around the country.

Buggying is an excellent complement to kitesurfing, and it is growing very quickly in popularity on many of the wide sandy beaches where riders are also found.

## Mountain boards

All terrain (ATB) or mountain boards are also a growing phenomenon; using them looks and feels very much like kitesurfing, and many riders are developing and refining their skills on these, especially when the water is cold. Using a mountain board is in fact harder than a kitesurfing board (I find!) because the steering linkage is dependent on the angle of the board. Many riders who are used to the water automatically react to the kite's pull by digging in their heels; the result is the board turns upwind and comes to a halt.

More advanced exponents may hook the harness line onto the buggy itself. This allows jumping and helps with power control, but it also means that you could find yourself being dragged down the beach in an inverted buggy with no way of releasing. This is why such devices are banned in most races.

There is a British association for buggy users. The Parakart Association is prin-

The basic technique is to steer the board by heel and toe pressure, while leaning back against the pull of the kite. The 'toe down, lean back' position this requires takes some practice, but once mastered the mountain board offers all the advantages of a small twin-tip on dry land, including the potential for huge airs!

Your kitesurfing kit is all compatible with using a landboard, so the additional expense of having a dry land alternative is minimal.

Helmets and pad sets are very strongly recommended for kite powered mountain boarding, a wipeout is likely to hurt more than at sea. If you are using your mountain board on sand, it is well worth washing it down after a session as the bearings and bolts do suffer from corrosion in salty conditions.

Roller blades, 2 and 4-wheeled karts and even regular skateboards can all be powered by kites.

The golden rules are: wear plenty of padding, and start with a small kite for the conditions and work up power in small increments.

## Snow kiting

Snow kiting with skis, snowboards or blades is growing rapidly in popularity. Till now all these glissade sports have relied on gravity for motive power, but with a traction kite and some wind, flat snowfields, frozen lakes, and even gentle upward slopes are no obstacle. (Some manufacturers and dealers think that the potential for snow kiting is even bigger than the waterborne variety.)

Like kitesurfers, the snowboys and girls are rapidly developing the potential for big airs and tricks.

If you are snow kiting then there are a few things to consider. Like buggies and all terrain boards, once away from the water a smaller ram-air kite is has some advantages over an inflatable. This is partially because of the better performance and handling, but also because tube kites are more prone to damage with land use and harder to 'pin down' on a slippery surface.

Open cell ram-air kites are perfect, but the normal de-power system on a bar is far more popular than the four-line handles often standard on kites of this type, as it gives excellent potential for jumps.

Because the wind is very often less smooth over land, the best choice is a model with large or valved cell openings that is resistant to turbulence. Some of the highest performing of the four- line race kites are a bit twitchy and prone to collapse in rough conditions.

Most closed-cell (valved) ram-air kites like the Flysurfer or Advance range work very well for both snow kiting and kitesurfing.

You will need a harness, of course. Many

Photo: www.extremesportphotos.com

surface it is a more secure connection.

Freestyle snowboards are the obvious choice of weapon, as they are controlled by heel and toe pressure just like a kiteboard and have the advantage of being twin-tipped. Skis take a little more effort to edge, as your feet are orientated fore and aft, requiring a sideways body lean to control the kite power. Wide skis have an advantage in this respect. Because they have relatively long rails, skis can be very efficient and fast once you get the hang of them.

If using conventional skis you will need to gybe, though riding backwards on twin tip freestyle skis is perfectly possible! Gybes are best done through a broad arc initially, keeping ground contact, but with a little practice good skiers can soon be making aerial turns.

A number of snowkiting schools are being set up in the prime areas, and snowkiting is a fast growing sector of the sport.

The resistance offered by hard snow or ice is tiny compared to water, so a moderate wind on flat ground requires a smaller kite than you need on water to get blasting. Once they have amassed some experience, some riders do choose bigger kites, making them radically over-powered - the reason for this is, of course, to give lift for big jumps!

snowkiters come from a different background to marine kitesurfers, and the use of climbing harnesses with a climbing karabiner to connect the chicken loop is not uncommon. This prevents handle-pass tricks and reduces your options to unhook, but for high boosts over a hard

If you undertake big jumps on windward

couple of kite boarders ripping diagonally upwards across the piste! Take care to give other slope users plenty of room and never cut across a busy slope. It will only take one ski school complaining to initiate a ban! Ski lifts, pylons and cables are perfectly designed to snare the unwary kite!

If you are off piste there are other hazards; you need to be careful to avoid hidden rocks and other obstacles, and if riding on virgin territory or deep snow you must be aware of hazards like tree holes, crevasses or hidden streams.

The combination of snow and wind means that losing body heat is a serious con-

Kites can be used for accessing extreme terrain and can be an aid to back-country touring.
*Photo: www.extremesportphotos.com*

slopes, be aware that the wind deflecting upward up the hill will give additional lift. This is huge fun when you know what you are doing, but could be dangerous if you find yourself at 25m up and climbing! (We can recommend a good book on paragliding if this is your thing!)

There are also extra safety considerations in snow kiting. In resorts there will be other skiers and boarders who will (yawn) only be expecting downhill traffic. It will be a shock to them to see a

cern when snow kiting. Hypothermia is a potential killer and you should never travel far without being well equipped for the conditions. Never ride alone, and if a few of you are out always ensure the slowest person is able to keep up.

If you are riding in remote back country areas, a mobile phone and a GPS are a big advantage and a necessity if you have a problem. Avalanche rescue equipment and knowledge are also strongly recommended. It could make the difference between life and death in the worst case scenario.

At speeds of 25mph you can cover a lot of ground, and if riding in the mountains

Who ever said that men can't multi-task?!
Photo: www.extremesportphotos.com

you need to also be aware of sudden drop-offs, snow cornices and sudden gusts or lulls that can be caused by the terrain. If you are riding over a frozen lake it is pretty obvious that it should have nice thick ice! (Otherwise you had better not slow down!)

Snow kiting has another element that is worth exploring - even if you go slow you will not (usually) sink. So just by adding a 3 or 4-metre rope you can easily tow another skier. (or kids on a sledge. Do keep checking over your shoulder, though, to make sure that you have not lost your passenger or gained an extra couple of kids!)

Ice skates, and toboggans can also be powered by kites, and treks in the Arctic or Antarctic (where kites have already been used) are obvious areas that could benefit from traction kite technology.

## Other water craft?

On water, kites can be used with water-skis (kite surfing in its earliest form!) and they can also be used for powering almost any small watercraft. They are particularly well suited to touring canoes, and have been used for dinghies or even a jetski that has packed up!

The rules of sailing dinghy races are tightly defined, so you cannot race with a kite; but as a parakart can almost double the speed of a conventional land yacht in light winds, due to the extra altitude of the kite and the ability to 'work it' for additional power, it is obvious that using a big kite on a sailing craft in weak conditions can make a big difference.

# How the Sport is Organised - the BKSA & IKO

The BKSA was set up in August '99. The aim of the organisation was, and still is, to promote the safe enjoyment of the sport in the UK.

The BKSA is run by an elected committee which has taken on the tasks of producing a training syllabus, arranging insurance cover for members and producing news updates which are distributed to the members (principally by e-mail). Instructor training, competitions and other events are also arranged by the BKSA, and it is the main channel of communication with other national bodies. It is recognised as the governing body of the sport in the UK by the Central Council for Physical Recreation (CCPR)

The BKSA is a stand-alone organisation, unlike some other national bodies such as the the French Flysurfing (Cerf Volante) organisation which is part of the FFVL (Federation Francaise de Vol Libre) which also oversees Hang-gliding and Paragliding and shares their insurance cover.

Many countries have developed national bodies, some like the FFVL and the BKSA are now well established and have produced training schemes and instruc-

tor rating programmes; others are simply a loose affiliation of riders and dealers.

In order to ensure that there are international standards for training and safety, and a recognised format for competitions, what was needed was an international network

to oversee member states and other groups, and to encourage new riders, dealers and instructors to aspire to membership.

At first the impetus for this came from manufacturers who were keen to offer a tie-in to some kind of qualified instruction with their product sales, and training programmes were offered by main dealers for certain brands, or were developed independently by companies who were already training windsurfing for example.. At the same time the international competition circuit was being developed, and the need for internationally recognised standards and rules was fast being recognised.

This was the background to the development of the IKO (International Kiteboarding Association) in 2001. The IKO is not independent - it is a commercial concern linked to a specific manufacturer, but it is true that some of the international links it helped to establish in countries with no strong association have proved a useful development. The IKO is principally concerned with promoting its own instructor certification and training courses, and has provided a platform for accrediting national and other qualifications that are widely recognised.

As the IKO became better known, various systems gradually integrated, so that most instructor qualifications worth having are now designed to meet the IKO standards and be ratified by them.

The IKO is run along the lines of a commercial organisation and does not have the status of a national governing body like the BKSA.

BKSA is still a young organisation and it is an uphill task to get the free spirits who typify this sport to join an association or pay good money to have insurance and admin work done. But, as has been proved by all the other adventure sports, from windsurfing to paragliding, a strong and effective governing body that can share information, arrange insurance and investigate accidents is vital.

Eventually government recognition and possibly funding for staff and training courses will be needed and the association needs support from all riders. It has already been the case that some council, landowner or other group of water users decide to try and ban kitesurfing from a lake or bay, and when that happens, a recognised national body, proper insurance and a set of international standards is needed to be able to make a strong case for us.

A club with an instructor holding an NVQ qualification, or a nationally recognised licence, is far more likely to be accepted by landowners, insurance companies, or other bodies, than a group of enthusiastic individuals.

The BKSA has thousands of members and a network of dozens of clubs in the UK.

Contact details are given in the information section of this book.

It is perfectly possible to be an individual rider and gain suitable insurance from your national or local association. However, most riders wish to ride with their mates - it is safer, more fun, and a better way to improve. The best way to do this is to join a local club. Many good kitesurfing venues have a club, and the riders are generally pretty friendly and keen to help newcomers. The BKSA website,

your national association or local instructor should be able to point you in the right direction.

Local advice on tides, the best spots in certain winds and the après-ride discussions in the beach bar are all good reasons to make contact!

As mentioned above, landowners and authorities find it much easier to deal with a club or group so that they can negotiate with a representative on issues such as no-go areas or beach access.

If the alternative is loads of expensive signage or chasing down individual riders to tell them not to use a certain bit of beach at busy times, the easy option is just to post a complete ban - a situation that has already occurred in some places. Responsible clubs are the key to our future freedom.

BKSA
222 The Seafront
Hayling Island
PO11 0AU, UK

e-mail: info@kitesurfing.org
Website: www.kitesurfing.org

# Buying Your Own Equipment

It would be foolish to recommend specific equipment, as the kites and boards are evolving so quickly. However, there are a few sensible guidelines that should help you make a decision.

As a novice, you are almost totally in the hands of the dealer who supplies you; you cannot realistically evaluate kit for yourself, and even magazine reviews are far from reliable (it is a fact of life that the magazines rely on advertising for their survival and they are unlikely to print a review slagging off a product from a major customer.)

Most riders will tell you that whatever they have got is the best thing, and anyhow very few have had the opportunity to try a wide range of kit.

That is the problem. The solution is simple. Take advice from a dealer you can trust (usually your instructor). Ideally they should offer a choice of products from different manufacturers.

If your first choice of dealer does not seem convincing, get a second opinion from another. I have found that while some dealers and instructors are a little narrow in their outlook and tend to favour one brand they are familiar with for example, they are almost without exception people who genuinely love the sport and who will give you the best advice they can.

The ideal solution is to do quite a bit of kitesurfing before buying anything, but as tuition and hire is expensive this may not be a practical option.

Choose a dealer who will demonstrate and let you fly the kite. Buying your first set of kit from a shop or a web site where you cannot get it out and play with it is generally a poor idea. A good dealer will give you some time explaining the setup and features of the kite you are buying. If you are buying as a beginner they should certainly ensure you have done, or are at the very least set up with a course before taking your cash!

Broadly speaking, a good plan for most new riders is a mid-aspect ratio kite that is easy to water re-launch as a first buy. These are not the highest performance models, but the two problems you will be facing as a novice are handling the kite in strong conditions and re-launching when you have fallen off, and these are the areas where mid-aspect ratio performance inflatables excel. The newest models with bridles - 'bow kites' - are well worth a look, as the flatter shape is more efficient, and the bigger de-power range means you will need fewer kites for a wide range of conditions.

Some closed cell ram-air kites are even easier to re-launch than these, especially in light conditions, but you must accept that if they do manage get drowned in deep water then there is no second chance, whereas you can mess about with

Board Rider: Dimitri Maramenides Photographer: John Carter

Typical mid-aspect ratio inflatable leading edge model.

an inflatable tube kite for half and hour and still re-launch it.

Another advantage of ram-air models is that they are great for snow kiting or land-boarding too. However, at the time of writing, most kite-schools and dealers still recommend the mid-aspect ratio inflatable as a safe first choice.

The very first commercially successful kite was the Wipika Classic, and this design is still the basis for the whole family of low aspect inflatables today, from a wide variety of manufacturers. If you start with a kite of this kind then chances are it will still hold a good trade in value when it is time to move on.

The quality of construction on many of the early models was surprisingly poor, considering the price. It has been quite common to spend hundreds of pounds on a kite, only to discover that the manual is two bits of photocopied paper or the valves simply do not work. The pumps provided could be inadequate or the critical wear points not reinforced.

Fortunately, competition is now so fierce that all the constructors are being forced to improve, but do have a close look, and always try inflating and flying the kite yourself rather than just reading the glossy adverts.

If you are buying used, make sure you check the kite fully pumped up and wait a while to ensure it is not leaking slowly. New bladders are easy to fit (see chapter 20) but they can be surprising hard to obtain. A customer looking for a replacement bladder for an older model from a leading manufacturer was recently told that he had to buy an entire set of six bladders, as single items were not available. This is hopeless service, so make sure you check spares are available when you buy.

What size? Well the truth is you need at least two, and preferably three kites to best use a good range of wind conditions, but assuming that most buyers will start with just one, the best advice is a medium-to-large model as the optimum choice. For an 85kg man using a low aspect ratio inflatable with a de-power system, that means a kite somewhere in the 12-16 square metre range. (See the notes on sizing kites below.) Of course this will be useless in very strong winds and poor in very light winds, but should do well enough in 14-20 knots which is the commonest range for kitesurfing.

A lighter rider at, say, 65kg will need to come down in size to somewhere in the 9-14m range.

These sizes are not applicable to closed cell ram-air kites, which are considerably more powerful. The size depends to a great extent on the de-power range available and some of the flatter 'bow' kites have a somewhat wider range.

A lot depends on the size of board you will be using, your physical strength and the prevailing winds in your location. You will need advice from your dealer.

## Kite sizing

There are three basic ways of measuring a kite: flat area, projected area, and a number made up by the manufacturer!

The flat area is simply the size of floor the kite covers when laid out.

The projected area is the size of the shadow of the inflated kite (given an infinitely distant light source). Or, to put in another way, it is the area you can see when you look up at the kite overhead.

The projected area is a much better indicator of the power that the kite will generate, and different designs may have the same flat area but quite different projected areas.

For example a small Flysurfer Pulse is almost flat, and a kite with 7m² of fabric has a projected are of almost 6m². An Airush Reactor 21m is very curved and a kite with 21m² of fabric may project an area of (say) only 13m². (These are arbitrary figures for illustration only). A Cabrinha Crossbow is less curved than the Reactor, but nowhere near as flat as the Flysurfer Pulse.

Different manufacturers use slightly different formulae to calculate the area of their kites, and sadly some do not even supply the actual projected area in their specification sheets.

As the sizes increase in a range the larger inflatable kites tend to be more curved, and therefore the ratio of flat to projected area becomes steadily further apart. For this reason it is common for the larger kites in a range to be truly enormous in order to generate a significant increase in power over their smaller brothers. The higher the aspect ratio of the kite the more pronounced this phenomenon.

A 12m low aspect ratio kite may have a greater projected area than a 15m high aspect ratio kite! Of course area is not the only measure of power - the speed is also crucial. A fast moving 10m kite is more efficient than a slow one, so those with a better de-power set-up or slimmer tubes will have a bigger power range.

A true airfoil section with a top and bottom surface is far more efficient than a

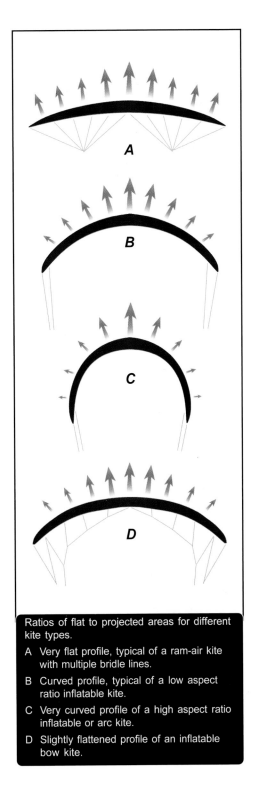

Ratios of flat to projected areas for different kite types.

A  Very flat profile, typical of a ram-air kite with multiple bridle lines.

B  Curved profile, typical of a low aspect ratio inflatable kite.

C  Very curved profile of a high aspect ratio inflatable or arc kite.

D  Slightly flattened profile of an inflatable bow kite.

single skinned foil, and this type of kite is built with far less curve, as they are usually supported by multiple bridle lines, so a 10m ram-air kite is equivalent in power to an inflatable of almost twice that (flat) area.

It is easy to see why you need specific and knowledgeable advice from your dealer or instructor!

## Boards

The next purchase is a board. This choice depends on where you will be riding. If it is on the sea, you will (usually) need to be able to cope with waves, and in this case a slightly longer board will make it easier. If you are lucky enough to have pretty smooth water, a shorter twin tip may be a good buy, but steer clear of wakeboards or very small boards until you have amassed quite a bit of experience.

If you are going to have to deal with bigger waves or surf, especially with onshore winds, you might want to think about a directional or a mutant board.

The bigger the width and area of the board, the easier to get planing in light winds, so for most new riders a fairly broad twin tip is the best choice - you can always go for a smaller board later (when the bigger model will still be handy for those light days).

## Harnesses

You will need a harness - of course, a regular windsurf seat or slalom harness can be used, although the bar position and buckles on some models may be poorly placed for kiting use. The latest kitesurf models are ideal, and have a handle on the back (very useful when being assisted) and a pocket to stash your hook knife, which are handy features.

Seated harness with rear handle

Waist harness

Waist harnesses are also popular, not least because they are the preferred choice of top riders doing airborne tricks, though some riders find it is a bit easier to control the power with a seat harness initially, and they do not ride up under the ribs, so they are a good choice for beginners, especially women.

## Clothing

The ideal situation is to be riding in the sun in a bikini or board shorts, though if it is that warm you will probably be well advised to wear a rash vest to prevent getting burnt! If you are riding in cool water you will need a good wetsuit. Even in water that you could happily swim in for several minutes, a wetsuit is a necessary piece of kit. The combination of wet skin and wind acts to reduce the apparent temperature very quickly, and it is no fun riding and very hard to learn while you are shivering.

### Wet suits

Wetsuits are available in a wide range of types to suit different temperatures. They work by trapping thin layer of water (or air) between your skin and the neoprene. If the gap is too big, this allows water to drain away and be replaced by a new batch of cold water, effectively cooling you down again. It is important that the suit fits snugly and the entry points at neck, arms and feet are well sealed.

This does not mean they should be really tight - a suit that limits the blood flow will also hasten cooling and can restrict free movement. It is important that the suits are tried on and allow a good range of movement, so it is worth taking your time when buying.

Shorties: these have short (or no) arms, and leg sections down to mid thigh. Typically made of 1 or 2mm. neoprene, they are useful to help maintain your core temperature in warmer water, and help combat any wind chill factor.

Rash vest

2mm shorty *(right)* and convertible wetsuit with arms off *(Photos: Gun)*

water entry.

NB: If it is really cold you will also need gloves and a neoprene hood. A good proportion of the body heat lost through wind chill is from your head.

Once in the shop and armed with a couple of plastic bags (to put on your feet to help slip the suits on), and knowing your likely riding conditions, there is a still a huge variety of suits and prices. What should you be looking for?

The quality of the neoprene fabric. This determines the useful life of the suit - basically the stretchier the better. Most suits use less stretchy material in areas like the chest and very flexible types for underarms, lumbar areas and shoulders, that are in constant motion. Titanium layered neoprene is more heat retentive and is used on some larger panels.

### Fit and flexibility

The suit should fit snugly, especially in the lower back and crotch areas, and it should be easy to bend your knees and elbows without causing bunching, which soon becomes uncomfortable. If short armed, the suit should allow for a bit of bicep bulge as you are sailing.

The next level is a 3mm suit with 2mm arms and legs. Many of these are convertibles, ie featuring detachable arms, giving you some scope to regulate your temperature. 4mm x 3mm suits are slightly warmer again, and are useful for extending your range of conditions.

Cold water and fresh winds demand a thicker suit. And a 'steamer' with a 5mm body and 3mm arms gives a good level of warmth in most spring and autumn conditions in the UK. Suits of this thickness are often semi-dry, meaning they are designed to work with almost no

The only area of the suit that can be very tight is the bit holding your belly in (for that James Bond look)!

### Seams

Seams are usually one of three types: the first, flatlocked, is the 'conventional' stitching system that is comfortable, strong and economical, but it does allow some water through the needle holes in the seams. Flatlock seams are sometimes taped to reduce this – they are best suited to summer suits.

Glued and blind stitched seams are those where the needle does not pass right through the fabric, giving a fully waterproof seam.

Some recent models on the market are not stitched at all, but use a welding technique to connect the panels.

### Water entry points

The sealing system at neck, ankle and wrist is very important, and winter semi-dry suits will use double seal systems. Neck seals can be very uncomfortable when the head is in constant motion - some kind of soft seal or flexible panel to minimise choke is a good idea - always try doing the suit right up and swivelling the head a few times to see how comfortable it is before buying!

Zips are the other main point of entry for water. As a general rule, vertical zippers are less waterproof than horizontal ones; new super stretchy fabrics allow many suits to have short zips or, in some cases, be completely zip free.

The neoprene is often laminated between layers of nylon; this makes it much more abrasion resistant and allows all sort sorts of colours to be added. However, the ny-lon does hold some water, which evaporates in the wind, draining heat, so a smoothskin suit with no external layer is warmer, though easier to damage.

For this reason uncoated panels are often used in the torso area, and are combined with regular nylon-coated varieties for areas of higher wear, such as arms and legs.

Black suits are a bit boring, they all look the same, and make you much less visible in the water; so smooth suits are appearing with colours and logos printed onto the surface. Time will tell how durable this will prove on a stretchy surface, but the 'silver surfer' look is now one step closer!

Neoprene consists of a cellular material with the principal insulation coming from the gas trapped inside the cells. As the suit gets older the gas gradually escapes and the suit slowly becomes less efficient. This is an inevitable process and means that older second hand suits will have suffered a significant degrading of performance by the time they are about 5 years old.

If you are riding in a shorty, 'surf slippers' will be fine for your feet. If the water is colder, you can get a reasonable

seal at the ankle by using boots and ensuring the wetsuit overlaps on top of the boots to prevent water draining into them.

If you can get everything from one place you may be able to do a deal. It is a fact of life that selling a package of training and equipment is better for the school than using all their kit. It is worth asking anyway!

## Headwear

A lot of heat is lost through the head, and a neoprene hat or cap can make a big difference when riding in cold weather. However, the preferred option is for a helmet, particularly where there are waves, as your board can surf around with a life of its own once you are off it, and getting cracked in the head by the nose of the board or a fin is a painful and potentially dangerous experience.

## Bouyancy aid

When you are water starting a flotation jacket of some sort (buoyancy aid) does make it a bit easier as you are higher in the water. They aid warmth as well, and they are very important if you face a long swim if you cannot re-launch your kite.

Any water buoyancy aid or life vest must give you full freedom of movement and not have any handles or buckles that could get trapped in the lines. Note that some waist harnesses cannot be used with some buoyancy aids as they obscure the hook.

There is now specialist kitesurfing clothing; the loose trousers and tops can be worn instead of or over the top of your wetsuit.

# Competitions

Kitesurfing is a sociable sport and competitions are a great excuse to get together with other kitesurfers, ride new venues and improve your skills. For the top riders it is an opportunity to test themselves against their peers and hopefully do well enough to pick up some sponsorship.

Competitions fall into three basic levels: local jams which are mostly for the crack and social benefits; national championships, which are still pretty relaxed but

are run in a professional manner for those who are keen on making their mark; and the international competition circuit, which is an important forum for pushing back the boundaries of what is possible, refining and demonstrating the latest equipment, and promoting the sport to a wider audience through TV and press coverage.

At the time of writing most kitesurf competitions are freestyle events - two or more riders competing head to head to do the best set, including their best moves and tricks. They are marked on difficulty and style.

Other specialist competitions include wave riding, hang-time (longest duration of a jump) and, of course, flat out racing.

The following is some of the competition data supplied by the BKSA in 2007.

Photo: F2 Kitesurfing

Photos: Tracey Kraft, Cabrinha

# BKSA 2007 GRAND PRIX SERIES

## Rule and Competition Summary

### General

Grand Prix rules may be reviewed and updated on an annual basis.

The Grand Prix series can be pre-registered by any rider wishing to compete in the series by contacting the BKSA. Priority will be given to these riders. Registration may also be done event by event on a first come first serve basis. Riders must be a member of the BKSA or another international organisation and hold the relevant insurance. Riders may join the BKSA on the day of competition.

## SAFETY & SPORTSMANSHIP ARE PARAMOUNT

### Race Format

There is no pre-set event programme and an information meeting will take place every day to inform riders of the programme. The event director and head judge will make the decision as to suitability of the conditions as to whether the competition commences or continues.

The BKSA race committee have the final decision as to which group a rider should compete in.

The BKSA Grand Prix is open to all nationalities.

There are no restrictions as to the type of sponsorship promotion on a rider's equipment, even if this is competition with the event sponsor. However, all riders must wear/ display if required promotion for the event sponsor and must not deface the said item – disciplinary measures will be taken.

All riders must be available for photos calls and interviews during the event. If riders do not comply they may be penalised with scores / prizes/ prize money being withheld.

### Rider Responsibility

Riders must use some kind of safely leash (min suicide leash) on kites and are advised to wear a helmet.

Each rider is responsible for making the decision on whether to start or remain in the competition.

It is there sole responsibility (or there guardian if 16 or under) to take the decision as to compete if they judge conditions to be beyond their skill level.

Each rider is personally liable for any damage to property or injury to a third party, which arises out of their equipment or their actions.

Riders may not enter the competition area, when not competing. If they do so they will receive one warning. A second infringement can result in the rider being disqualified from the competition.

Each rider will perform as an individual, but may be helped to land and launch on the beach , any rider helped while competing ie relaunch of kite, board recovery will be disqualified from heat while in the competition box. Once outside this area kites may be relaunched , boards recovered and riders assisted by third parties.

Any rider must help another rider if they are in danger and they are capable of doing so. A heat may be re run if it is deemed necessary.

## Classes

There will be a maximum of 24 riders in each class.

Grand Prix classes as follows

### Pro Fleet, Men, Women.

Pro Men and ladies class is completed by riders who compete as professionals; defined as those receiving sponsorship by the industry to compete.

Except- Members of the trade who receive kit as part of there job can be in amateur/ladies as decided by race committee.

### Mens and Ladies  Amateurs (Ams 14 - 34)

Can include shop sponsored riders but not industry.

### Seniors

Defined as 35 or over ( on the 1/1/07)

### Juniors

Defined as 16yrs or under (on the 1/1/07), will compete together. The class is mixed male and female.

Juniors can compete in pro fleet or amateur fleets as long as they have there guardians written permission to do so and the Race Director and Head Judge are satisfied with the riders competence level and ability.

The Junior may not compete in another fleet other than the one decided upon.

A minimum of 2 competitors per class is required to run an official round. There will be a maximum of 24

## Competition

Any rider surfing dangerously or being verbally abusive will face verbal and or written warnings. Depending on the seriousness of the offence they can face disqualification from the heat, round or championships.

Riders will be informed of specifics, alterations or additions to these rules, at the daily meeting.

All start times; heat durations and flag signals will be covered at the daily briefing meet if in doubt ask the beach marshal

Visual signals may be accompanied by an acoustic signal, but only the visual signal count.

Each rider will compete as indicated on the scoreboard and shall be solely responsible for competing in the right heat at the right time.

If the head judge does not deem a competitor to be up to standard or they are unsafe, they will not be allowed to continue.

A minimum of two riders will take part in each heat and will be judged by overall impression, taking into consideration:

1.   **Technical Difficulty**
2.   **Height**
3.   **Smoothness**
4.   **Power**
5.   **Style.**

Judges will take the following taken into account:

### 1. Jumps

Jumps on both sides, number of rotations, type of rotation, back, front, off axis, handlepass, kiteloops. Jumps are defined by the airtime and continuing in the same direction.

### 2. Tricks

Low level ·one hand, board take offs, handle passes, blindside, switch, grabs, the total fluidity and style of the manoeuvre.

### 3. Transitions

A jump or trick will be scored as a transition when the move is started in one direction and landed in another.

### 4. Landing

Three types:

a) Perfect landing when the board touches the water first, the jump/trick will score maximum

b) Water start landing when your bum touches the water and the board is sliding. The jump/trick may only score a potential of 50%.

c) Slam landing when the back of the rider hits the water before the board or the rider sinks and does not plane away. The jump/trick scores 0.

### 5. Crashed and lost kites/boards

These will be noted as potential tiebreakers.

Riders can only be scored in the competition area, for what the judges see, not for what competitors think they have done.

The rider coming in must move away from the rider coming out from the shore. If neither is going in or out, then the starboard tack rider has priority.

When overtaking kites must be raised or lowered accordingly and the upwind rider move away from the downwind.

In waves, the rider who is at the peak has priority.

Riders may not change course to hinder another rider.

All competitors must keep clear of capsized riders. No penalties will be given against a rider who collides with another rider who capsizes directly in front of them.

### Handle Passes

When riders are on the same reach only the rearward downwind rider can pull a handlepass. This is to avoid complications if the front rider gybes or transitions without looking if another rider is behind him.

When riders are on opposite reaches only the downwind rider can pull a handle pass. This is to avoid dangerous riding in front of an oncoming rider.

Riders will be penalised if the judges feel there was not enough room for safe execution of the trick.

Do not pull handle passes in Onshore winds closer than 100M from the judging point

Handle pass leashes must be worn at all times. Do not handle pass if in doubt – think safety.

There is a no-protest rule in place for the BKSA Grand Prix Series.

All instructions issued by safety crews on water or land must be undertaken immediately.

## Scoring and Prizemoney

The Grand Prix ( Pro fleet ) format will be freestyle, progressed through single eliminator heats. Other competition formats may take place dependant upon conditions and time available these too will count towards your scores.

The Amateur men/ladies and Juniors format will be freestyle , progressed through single elimination or expression type sessions depending on time and conditions.

The empahssis is on fun and time on the water, a more informal competition format may be used.

### Pro Mens and Ladies-

There will be an overall champion for the year made up all scores from all rounds ( both freestyle and other comp formats from the 5 events ). Only one round of freestyle and one other comp format will be counted at each event.

### Amateur mens/ladies , seniors  and Junior

Will be decided on the best 5 results/scores of the Year.

Each individual event will be calculated on all the results at that event and points and prizemoney awarded as follows

| Position | Points | Freestyle | | Points | Second Discipline | |
|---|---|---|---|---|---|---|
| | | Prize money | | | Prize money | |
| | | Men | Ladies | | Men | Ladies |
| 1st | 1000 | 30% | 30% | 400 | 30% | 30% |
| 2nd | 860 | 20% | 20% | 344 | 20% | 20% |
| 3rd | 730 | 10% | 10% | 292 | 10% | 10% |
| 4th | 670 | | | 268 | | |
| 5th | 610 | | | 244 | | |
| 7th | 556 | | | 226 | | |
| 9th | 500 | | | 226 | | |
| 13th | 452 | | | 200 | | |
| 17th | 400 | | | 180 | | |
| 25th | 360 | | | 160 | | |

In the event of only freestyle taking place all prizemoney will be given to that discipline. In the event of Freestyle and another comp taking place the prize fund will be split $^2/_3$ to Freestyle and $^1/_3$ to the other discipline.

In the event of no freestyle and another comp formats taking place the points will be scored and counted as a second discipline and the prize fund will be paid to that one discipline

Reportages may take place if time allows, we want to make sure we complete the rounds. There may be some 'byes' due to insufficient numbers, these will be given to higher ranked riders based on previous results.

Riders can register for events and miss rounds if for a valid reason they cannot make days of competition due to work or family commitments. In this case they will receive max points for the day as long as entry fee is paid in full. If a round has not been started and they arrive they will be allowed to enter as long as they have pre registered and informed the race crew.

Points will be awarded in the event of no comp taking place according to the number of riders registered – these will count to the overall championships. Therefore if no comp takes place and 13 riders register 452 points will be awarded

In the event of no comp, any prize fund after other funds have been paid for (such as best trick comp or registration shortfall) will be subdivided between pro riders.

## Prize Giving

This will normally be made approximately ½ hour after the end of the comp or at a time posted on the official notice board – all riders to attend, usually held at the Judging tower.

## THROUGHOUT THE COMPETITION SAFETY & SPORTSMANSHIP ARE PARAMOUNT.

# Becoming an Instructor

If you have been riding for a while, are competent in a range of conditions and a good communicator, then you may be tempted to try your hand at instructing the sport yourself.

The sport is growing quickly and there is a steady demand for new instructors.

The British Kite Surfing Association run instructor training courses, examines candidates and award qualifications to those reaching the required standard to be a BKSA instructor.

Outside the UK there are other bodies that award their own instructional qualifications, all are broadly similar in content, though the BKSA standard is widely recognised as setting a high standard of professionalism.

Passing the course and examination is down to the judgment of the assessor.

The entry criteria to attend a BKSA instructor course are as follows.

## Equipment Knowledge Requirements

### Kites

1. To be fully familiar with all the equipment that he/she uses for training members of the public

2. To know how to adjust and tune the equipment for varying levels of performance

3. To know when equipment needs repairing and how to have it repaired accordingly

4. To be able to select the correct kite, lines

and control gear for prevailing wind and weather conditions, both for themselves and for their students

5. To fully understand all aspects of line management including knots used, line care, unwinding lines, storing lines, the dangers of lines moving through the air and adrift at sea

6. To understand and be able to explain the theory of traction kite aerodynamics

### Kiteboard & Other Equipment

1. To be fully familiar with all the equipment that he/she uses for training members of the public

2. To know how to adjust and tune the equipment for varying levels of performance

3. To know when equipment needs repairing and to have it repaired accordingly

4. To be able to select the correct board, fins, straps, harness, wetsuit for prevailing wind and weather conditions, both for themselves and for their students

5. To understand and be able to explain the theory of fluid and board dynamics.

## Flying Skills Requirements

### Land

1. To know how to launch a kite in any wind condition (aided and unaided)

2. To know how to land a kite in any wind condition (aided and unaided)

3. To be in full control (within reason) of the kite at all times

4. To know how to handle the kite in an emergency and during freak gusts

### Water

1. To be able to kitesurf competently upwind, crosswind and downwind in both directions

2. To be able to kitesurf effectively and efficiently and have the ability to sail a board in reasonable conditions, putting it safely and competently anywhere.

## Personal Qualities required

- Enthusiasm
- Communication skills
- Patience
- Organisational skills
- Decisiveness
- Good judgment
- Sense of humour

## Administration Requirements

1. To keep a detailed accident log book

2. To keep detailed records of all courses given including attendees personal information, levels of proficiency achieved, course dates, weather conditions

3. To have instructor indemnity insurance to a value of £2,000,000, third party liability.

4. To be able to supply certificates to attendees who complete the course that reflects the level of their achievement

5. To have permission from all relevant local organisations to hold kitesurfing lessons in that area

## Safety Requirements

### General

1. To fully understand the BKSA safety regulations and to be able to implement them along with the safety equipment specified by the BKSA for themselves and for course attendees

2. To fully understand 'The Seven Common Senses' - These are safety considerations that have been adapted from the windsurfing recommendations compiled by the Royal Yachting Association (RYA). The BKSA are happy

to take advantage of the RYA's many years of experience in teaching all kinds of watersports and to adapt these as its own recommendations.

These are listed in Chapter 4, Health and Safety

## Wind

1. To understand the power of the wind and to anticipate dangerous situations

2. To understand wind direction and how it affects Kitesurfers direction, including the dangers of off shore winds

3. To be aware that freak gusts can occur and to know how to respond to them

4. To know the difference between being under-powered and over-powered and to know what equipment to use to be correctly powered

## Water

1. To know and understand that a Kitesurfer is classed as a sailing vessel and should conduct itself according to the International Rules for Preventing Collisions at Sea (IRPCS)

2. To be aware of the potential dangers of the sea, including tides, undercurrents and poor visibility

3. To assess local water hazards, such as rocks, groyns, coral, sand banks etc.

Effectively this means that you will have had to spent a considerable amount of time assisting at an existing school helping qualified instructors, and building your own training experience, prior to attending your own course and being assessed.

## Qualifications Requirements

1. To have a minimum of RYA level 2 Powerboat Certificate (and preferably to have level 3) – this can be upgraded at a later stage

2. To have an officially recognised First Aid certificate

3. To have attended the relevant National Coaching Foundation course (background in coaching basics)

4. To have passed a BKSA instructor training course

The exact standards and acceptable qualifications are determined by the BKSA and course assessor, the riding standards in particular will become more exacting as demand for courses grows.

The first instructors were training using just 2 line kites and directional boards.

Now de-power systems, ram air kites and twin tip boards are entailing a much broader knowledge base for candidates.

All the knowledge and qualifications above do not make a good instructor, in order to teach well you need to have an ability to understand the needs of each student, some may be nervous and require lots of help and encouragement, some may be over-keen and need holding a back a little to perfect one element before rushing on to the next.

In many adventurous or extreme sports it is natural that people who are very competent themselves become instructors, this is a good thing, but they must also be capable of putting themselves in the position of students who may be less naturally co-coordinated!

Teaching kitesurfing well is not an easy task, the nature of the sport means that quite a few things are happening at once, and breaking it down into easy to master portions can be challenging. Not only that, but as soon as your student begins to get the idea they are moving away from you! It requires a sharp eye for detail to see the important points they need to work on. Possibly the toughest challenge though is teaching in variable conditions or waves.

Good conditions are vital to make reasonable progress for most students. This means having the benefits of shallow water and consistent winds. Getting both in the UK is good going; getting warm water as well generally means buying a plane ticket!

Having watched a number of kitesurfing instructors at work, it is apparent that those that do the best job are always those who use all the range of "tools" available to them, whether it is demonstrating a skill, de-briefing clearly, or simply telling a story to illustrate an important point. If they get cold or tired pupils stop progressing and, more importantly stop enjoying the experience. So the instructors' brief includes structuring the lessons to deal with this.

A senior instructor may wish to run their own outfit and perhaps apply for recognition by the BKSA. The schools that have done this have also needed to satisfy the association with their risk assessments, training venues and equipment and administrative skills.

Unless it has the benefit of a shallow body of water, the school will need a rescue craft of some kind, and the instructor requirements above require basic boat handling competence. (The rescue craft may well be a jetski, (of the sit-on wetbike type) which are easy to use and have the advantage of no external propeller for mangling floating lines.

Kitesurf instructors do not get rich! but there is a good deal of satisfaction from teaching people a new skill and doing something you enjoy, if you think it may be for you then try contacting your local school and if they think you have the right stuff they will help you jump through all the hoops to become a qualified instructor.

Not like that - like this!

# The State of the Art, Innovations and the Future

The first few years of the sport has seen great progress in the standards of instruction and the organisation of the sport in many countries, but the outstanding area of change has been in the equipment itself.

On my own first attempt (in '98) the Wipika classic 2-line kite was the dominant model and there were only large directional boards or wakeboards available.

The same year the Flexifoil boys crossed the channel with Blades (ram-air open cell kites), which was a phenomenal achievement and publicity coup, but there was no association, no proper competition circuit and no magazines!

Right now we have a huge diversity of gear

...some of the present weaknesses of the gear will be solved by technical innovation...
(Photo: www.extremesportphotos.com)

and things are still changing quickly. Many manufacturers, including windsurfing and paragliding manufacturers, have joined the market, bringing a wealth of related knowledge, and the snow kiting scene is just beginning to get really hot!

So what of the future? It may be completely wrong, but it is fun to speculate on what may happen....

A really fast, efficient kite with a huge de-power range that will water re-launch every time is the holy grail. We are much closer now than five years ago and the technology can only continue to improve. A good example is the quick release kite leashes that are almost universal now and which could have prevented many of the accidents suffered by early riders. Their adoption has made the sport far safer.

Kitesurfing will discover speed trials, and it is possible that really fast kites based on single skin hang-gliders or windsurf sail technology will revolutionise the speeds we can attain.

Boards will gradually become more specialised, with speed boards, jumping boards and boards that are superb upwind - maybe these last will be convex in section, with the rail in the water designed to be vertical at full speed, or have a daggerboard that can be deployed for much better upwind progress.

Kiteboarders at the cutting edge are still inventing new moves; there are kiteboarders getting 'tubed' in big waves like conventional surfers, and new course racing tasks are being set at some competitions.

The real use of kite technology, however, is not directly for kitesurfing as a sport at all, but in the use of kites for larger craft. There is big money in open ocean yacht racing and even more in commercial shipping. Kites have a big future in these fields!

In kitesurfing as a sport, I am sorry to say I expect there to be some more serious accidents as more and more people get involved. I personally know of riders who have been dragged up a beach and hit a parked car, been blown over a 20ft cliff, hit a coral reef at speed, and gone for a sub-surface drag with a line wrapped around a foot. All these have got away with it, but others have not, and there have been fatalities..

Most accidents can be avoided with good training and a sensible attitude to weather and personal abilities. The way of the world is that sooner or later a student at a kitesurf school, or a swimmer who gets injured by a board, will sue their instructor or the guy on the board for a million pounds for a nasty head injury or worse, and insurance and access to public areas will become even hotter issues than now.

Effective national organisations like the BKSA and, particularly, properly run local schools and clubs are the best way to ensure our sport can grow safely.

The competitions are already proving a big hit with the satellite and cable TV companies, as they are very photogenic; kitesurfing has featured in car ads and is all over outdoor clothing stores such as Fat Face.

If a major event makes terrestrial prime time TV, then kitesurfing could get a big boost.

It is likely that snow kiting will continue to grow quickly. The biggest problem is that snow and wind together make a pretty cold and unpleasant environment. This is likely to limit the mass appeal.

In other sports, such as paragliding, sailing, or climbing, there has been a bit of a divergence with racing people, freestyle people and expedition people.

Right now everything is freestyle based, but pure speed is a big attraction. The expedition element has hardly been explored in kitesurfing, although Manu Bertin, the original pioneer of the sport, has recently managed to kite across the Atlantic Ocean using a mixture of a small inflatable boat, a regular board and a thing that looks like a buggy mounted on two windsurf boards!

Perhaps 'safaris' like this around island chains, or coast lines, or perhaps expeditions that are part buggying, part kitesurfing or part snow kiting, will catch the public's attention, maybe it will be you doing it? I look forward to watching the sport continue to develop and reading the articles!

Ride safely, see you on the water.

Is this the future...!?
*(Photo: www.extremesportphotos.com)*

# Information

## National Associations

### British Kitesurfing Association, BKSA

**Communication with the BKSA:**

- They are an internet based organisation

- For general enquiries/questions email: info@kitesurfing.org

- If you want to speak to someone they have a 5 day-a-week office number for most queries 0044 (0)1305 813555 or a mobile number 00 44 (0)7980 553057

- Website: http://www.kitesurfing.org
  *(The website has links to many of the others listed below)*

- Address:  BKSA
  222 The Seafront
  Hayling Island
  PO11 0AU, UK

The BKSA was set up in August '99. The aim of the organisation is to promote the safe enjoyment of the sport in the UK.

The BKSA is currently engaged in setting up a training syllabus, arranging insurance cover for members and producing news updates which are presently being distributed principally by e-mail. Instructor training, competitions and other events will be arranged by the BKSA, and it will be the main channel of communication with other national bodies.

## Other National Governing Bodies

**AUSTRALIA**

Australian Kitesurf Association

Website: www.aksa.com.au

**BELGIUM**

Website: www.kitesurfing.be

**FRANCE.**

Federation Francaise de Vol Libre

(FFVL)
4 Rue de Suisse
06000 Nice
France

Tel: 04 07 03 82 82

Website: www.ffvl.fr

**GERMANY**

German Kitesurf Association

Website: www.gksa.de

**GREECE**

Greek Kitesurf Association

Website: www.gwa.gr

**ITALY**

Italian Kitesurf Association

Website: www.fki.it

**SPAIN**

Spanish Kitesurfing Association (AEK)

Website: www.e-pale.com/AEK/

**USA**

United States Kitesurfing Association (USKA)

Website: www.e-uskite.org

**INTERNATIONAL**

IKO: The International Kiteboarding Organisation.

The IKO is a company that has two roles, one, like the BKSA is in arranging training, qualifying instructors etc. The other is as a profit making venture, selling their own publications and with a commercial tie-in to one manufacturer (Starkites). This is sometimes an uneasy mix, but the IKO has been very useful in providing a framework for those areas or countries which do not have an association of their own.

Website: www.ikointl.com

**ONLINE TRAINING INFORMATION**

Interesting website with lots of useful tips and techniques etc.

Website:
www.netcom.ca/~hungvu/kitesurfing.htm

# Weather and Tides

**UK Weather Forecasts**

Websites:    www.bbc.co.uk/weather
             www.met-office.gov.uk

**UK Inshore Waters Forecast**

Website:
www.bbc.co.uk/weather/ship_inshore.shtml

**UK actual weather subscription service.**

Website: www.wendywindblows.com

**USA Weather**

Website: www.windcall.com

**France/European coastal weather**

Website: www.meteo.fr/marine/cote

**Tide Data UK**

Websites:    www.tidetimes.co.uk
             www.uktides.com

**Tide Data US**

Websites: www.tidesonline.com

# On Wheels

**Mountainboards/ATB's**

Website: www.ATBsports.co.uk

**Buggies/parakarts.**

British Power Kitesports Association

Website: www.bpka.co.uk

# On Snow

General snowkiting site

Website: www.snowkiting.com

# Directory of BKSA Schools

The following directory listings are listed alphabetically. The number next to each listing can be referenced to the number on the map below. The BKSA website has an up-to-date and definitive list of BKSA approved schools.

| **1** | **Airzone** |
|---|---|

| Address: | The Stables Lychgate Green Titchfield Fareham Hampshire PO14 3LL | Tel: | 01329 665842 or 07973 891335 |
|---|---|---|---|
| | | email: | lessons@kitesurfUK.com |
| | | web: | www.kitesurfUK.com |
| | | Services: | ■ ▨ ■ |

| About: | Fully qualified and insured BKSA / IKO accredited instructor. Learn the basics in 1 day - get going on the water in 3. |
|---|---|

**KEY**

■ School  □ Shop  ■ Venue  □ Distributor

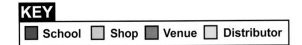

## 2   Atlantic Riders School

| | |
|---|---|
| Contact: | Will Bennet |
| Address: | Boswiddle |
| | Ladock |
| | Truro |
| | Cornwall |
| | TR2 4NU |

Tel: 07791 937207
email: info@atlanticriders.co.uk
web: www.atlanticriders.co.uk
Services: ■ ■

**BKSA** Approved Shool

**About:** Based at Watergate Bay, a school for Beginners, intermediates, and gifted riders wanting to be pushed beyond their own expectations. Strapless riding specialists.

## 3   Easyriders Kiteboarding

| | |
|---|---|
| Contact: | Andy Gratwick |
| Address: | 89 Salterns Road |
| | Whitecliff |
| | Poole |
| | Dorset |
| | BH14 8BL |

Tel: 01202 731763 or 07980 577893
email: info@easyriderskiteboarding.com
web: www.easyriderskiteboarding.com
Services: ■ □ ■

**BKSA** Approved Shool

**About:** Based at Poole harbour - one of the largest and most beautiful natural harbours in the world. Tuition & Surf safaris.

## 4   Big Blue Kite School

| | |
|---|---|
| Contact: | Oli Tugggey |
| Address: | c/o Newsurf |
| | Newgale |
| | Haverfordwest |
| | Pembrokeshire |
| | SA62 6AS |

Tel: 07816 169359 or 07970 034535
email: info@bigbluekitesurfing.com
web: www.bigbluekitesurfing.com
Services: ■ □ ■

**BKSA** Approved Shool

**About:** Professional kitesports tuition and holidays in the Pembrokeshire coast national park. Beginners and advanced. New & second hand equipment.

## 5   Essex Kitesurf School

| | |
|---|---|
| Contact: | Simon Mudd |
| Address: | 36 Manor Rd |
| | Benfleet |
| | Essex |
| | SS7 4BG |

Tel: 07751 705558
email: sxmail@tiscali.co.uk
web: www.essexkitesurfschool.co.uk
Services: ■ □ ■

**BKSA** Approved Shool

**About:** BKSA/ IKO Approved school, Beginner to advanced tuition. All equipment supplied. 1 Hour from London to Shoeburyness station.

## 6   FKS Kitesurf School

| | |
|---|---|
| Address: | 7 Marine Terrace |
| | Rhosneigr |
| | Anglesey |
| | North Wales |
| | LL64 5UQ |

Tel: 01407 810598 or 07876 338952
email: Bucky@funsport.fsnet.co.uk
web: www.buckys.co.uk
Services: ■ □ ■

**BKSA** Approved Shool

**About:** Windsurfing and water sport shop, mainly dealing in windsurfing, kite surfing and surfing accessories. Kitesurf tuition and sales.

## 7   Gower Kiteriders

| Contact: | Matt Smith | Tel: | 01792 367453 or 07799 062447 |
| --- | --- | --- | --- |
| Address: | 11 Clifton Terrace<br>Mumbles<br>Swansea<br>SA34EJ | email:<br>web:<br>Services: | info@gowerkiteriders.com<br>www.gowerkiteriders.com |

**About:**    London-Swansea –3hrs      Birmingham-Swansea-2hr30      Bristol-Swansea-1hr20

## 8   Hayling Island Kitesurf School

| Contact: | Chris Bull | Tel: | 023 92422 570 or 07956 125870 |
| --- | --- | --- | --- |
| Address: | 28 Blackthorn Rd<br>Hayling Island<br>Hampshire<br>PO11 9NY | email:<br>web:<br>Services: | info@hikitesurfschool.co.uk<br>www.hikitesurfschool.co.uk |

**About:**    Hayling Island is 5 miles from Portsmouth (London 1hr 15). It boasts some of the best kitesurfing conditions in the UK, with over a kilometer of flat shallow water.

## 9   Kite Sports (Scotland) Ltd

| Contact: | Bob Yull | Tel: | 07875 773346 |
| --- | --- | --- | --- |
| Address: | St Andrews<br>Fife<br>Scotland | email:<br>web:<br>Services: | info@kss.uk.com<br>www.kss.uk.com |

**About:**    Scotland's premier kite sports training centre. We primarily focus on kitesurfing, but we still offer tuition in all aspects of kite flying.

## 10   Mobius Kite School

| Contact: | Louise McDonagh<br>Tim Ovens | Tel:<br>email: | 01637 831383<br>info@mobiusonline.co.uk |
| --- | --- | --- | --- |
| Address: | 17 Churchfields Rd<br>Cuber<br>Cornwall<br>TR8 5JN | web:<br>Services: | www.mobiusonline.co.uk |

**About:**    Location: Perranporth (Nr Newquay), Hayle/The Bluff (Nr St Ives), Marazion (Nr Penzance), Pentewan (Nr St Austell) plus other locations.

## 11   Paracademy

| Contact: | Spence Whyte | Tel: | 01305 824797 |
| --- | --- | --- | --- |
| Address: | The Old Scuba Centre<br>Masonic Carpark<br>Victoria Square<br>Portland<br>Dorset, DT5 1AL | email:<br>web:<br>Services: | info@paracademy.co.uk<br>www.paracademy.co.uk |

**About:**    The UK´s leading power kite sports centre

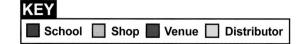

**KEY**

■ School ■ Shop ■ Venue □ Distributor

---

## 12   Rye Watersports

| | | |
|---|---|---|
| **Contact:** | Maragaret, Rosie, George | **Tel:**    01797 225238 or 07939 484840 |
| **Address:** | North Point Water <br> New Lydd Rd <br> Camber <br> Rye, E. Sussex, TN31 7QS | **email:**   team@ryewatersports.co.uk <br> **web:**    www.ryewatersports.co.uk <br> **Services:**   ■ ■ ■ |

**About:**   The premier kitesurfing school in the south east, only 1hr from the M25. Lake based tuition on safe, flat water.

---

## 13   Synergy Kitesports

| | | |
|---|---|---|
| **Contact:** | Mark Davies | **Tel:**    01224 638868/07981 793066 |
| **Address:** | 122 Seamount Court <br> Aberdeen <br> AB25 1DS | **email:**   maggieandmark@hotmail.co.uk <br> **web:**    www.synergykitesports.co.uk <br> **Services:**   ■ ■ ■ |

**About:**   We offer tuition, coaching and equipment sales, in all kitesports in Aberdeen and throughout North East Scotland.

---

## 14   Torquay Kitesurfing & Kitebuggying School

| | | |
|---|---|---|
| **Contact:** | Andre Shorland | **Tel:**    01803 212411 |
| **Address:** | 55 Victoria Rd <br> Ellacombe <br> Torquay <br> Devon, TQ1 1HX | **email:**   torquaykitesurf@tiscali.co.uk <br> **web:**    www.kitesurfing-torquaywindsurfing.co.uk <br> **Services:**   ■ ■ ■ |

**About:**   BKSA and IKO approved school for Kitesurfing. BBC qualified for Kite Buggying. Shop stocks comprehensive range of equipment inc used equipment

---

## 15   Transition Kiteboarding

| | | |
|---|---|---|
| **Address:** | 96 Greenvale Rd <br> London <br> SE9 1PF | **Tel:**    020 8378 2138 <br> **email:**   info@transitionkiteboarding.com |
| **Teaching:** | 1 Beach Walk <br> Whitstable <br> Kent, CT5 2BP | **web:**    www.transitionkiteboarding.com <br> **Services:**   ■    ■ |

**About:**   Range of courses including kite surfing lessons from introductory to advanced courses, as well as land boarding lessons, snow kiting and parakarting.

---

## 16   X-Isle Sports (UK)

| | | |
|---|---|---|
| **Contact:** | Rob Pigot | **Tel:**    01983 873111 <br>         07966 476163 |
| **Address:** | UK Wipika Kiteboard Ctr <br> Bembridge Boatyard <br> Embankment Road <br> Isle of Wight, PO35 5NR | **email:**   info@x-is.co.uk <br> **web:**    www.x-is.co.uk <br> **Services:**   ■ ■ ■ |

**About:**   X-Isle was formed in 2002 and is now one of the UK's premier watersports companies operating from Silver Beach, Bembridge, Isle of Wight, UK and Nyali Beach, Mombasa, Kenya.

## 17 | X-Train

| Address: | West Wittering Estate<br>West Wittering<br>Chichester<br>West Sussex<br>PO20 8AJ | Tel:<br>email:<br>web:<br>Services: | 01243 513077<br>info@x-train.co.uk<br>www.x-train.co.uk<br>■ ▢ ■ |
| --- | --- | --- | --- |

**BKSA** Approved Shool

| About: | Kitesurfing Windsurfing and Surfing. We are a fully certified BKSA and RYA centre and have been teaching Kitesurfing for 5 years at West Wittering beach. |
| --- | --- |

# Organisations not recognised by the BKSA

## Airhead Boardsports

| Address: | 26 Churchill Parade<br>Rustington<br>W. Sussex<br>BN16 3DE | Tel:<br>email:<br>web:<br>Services: | 01903 850831<br>info@air-head.com<br>www.air-head.com<br>■ ▢ |
| --- | --- | --- | --- |

| About: | The one stop Exteme Sports shop !! Airhead has a large range of equipment, surf brands and accessories with Mail Order and On-Line store. |
| --- | --- |

## Oceanside

| Address: | 8 Southend Rd<br>Hunstanton<br>Norfolk<br>PE36 5AW | Tel:<br>email:<br>web:<br>Services: | 01485 534455<br>info@oceanside.co.uk<br>www.oceanside.co.uk<br>■ ▢ ■ ▢ |
| --- | --- | --- | --- |

| About: | Shop and school on the east coast. Online shop and informative website. Importer of Flysurfer kites. |
| --- | --- |

## Poole Harbour Boardsailing

| Contact: | Chris Shaw/Karl Cadwallader | Tel: | 01202 700503 |
| --- | --- | --- | --- |
| Address: | 284 Sandbanks Rd<br>Poole<br>Dorset, BH4 8HU | email:<br>web:<br>Services: | info@pooleharbour.co.uk<br>www.pooleharbour.co.uk<br>■ ▢ ■ |

| About: | All brands of kitesurfing equipment are available to us. We also provide tuition with IKO qualified instructors and give you a free day long lesson with your first kite and board purchase. |
| --- | --- |

## Western Isles Kite Company

| Contact: | David Hepworth | Tel: | 01851 672771/07854 754523 |
| --- | --- | --- | --- |
| Address: | West View<br>Aird of Uig<br>Isle of Lewis, HS2 9JA | email:<br>web:<br>Services: | info@powerkitesales.co.uk<br>www.wikc.co.uk<br>■ ▢ ■ |

| About: | B&B acommodation, unique location, training in all kitesports, Ozone & Gin specialists Thundercat RIB support. BKSA/ IKO/ BPKA instructors. |
| --- | --- |

## Winddesigns Ltd

| Address: | Unit 5, Century Park<br>Lynn Rd<br>Chettisham<br>Ely, Cambs<br>CB6 1SA | Tel:<br>email:<br>web:<br>Services: | +44 (0)870 870 6065<br>sales@wind-designs.com<br>www.wind-designs.com<br>▢ |
| --- | --- | --- | --- |

| About: | One of the UK's leading distributors of kiting products. |
| --- | --- |

## WHAT THE BKSA DO

Access - **Keeping beaches open**

Teaching - **Setting the standards of teaching in the UK**

Instructors - **Training of instructors**

Schools - **Inspecting, Approving the BKSA schools network**

Events - **Running the National championships**

Clubs - **Helping set up and run clubs throughout the UK**

We work with many national organisations, councils, local authorities and landowners to ensure that the sport is understood ,taught and practised in safety.

### *Your membership also gives you...*

- 3rd Party liability insurance worlwide (to value of £5m) whilst flying any kite on water/land, kitesurfing, kitelandboarding, snowkiting, buggying and powerkiting
- The right and correct insurance to compete in any BKSA approved event
- A membership card and joining pack
- One vote at AGM meetings
- Regular newsletters - via email
- Membership is open to any nationality, not just British

#### *For UK Residents only!*

You can also join an affiliated Kite Surf Club (some clubs may charge more depending on membership benefits) for just an additional £5 per annum .

***You can pay using nearly any of the major credit or debit cards.***

## Join online today www.kitesurfing.org

www.KiteboardingUK.com
www.KiteboardingUKshop.com
www.KiteboardingUKforum.com

Email: info@kiteboardinguk.com
301 London Road South

ahead of its time

FLYSURFER the No.1 with foilkites.

# Glossary

### Anemometer

An instrument for measuring wind speed.

### Angle of attack

The angle between the airflow and the chord line of the aerofoil. The angle of attack determines the amount of lift produced by the kite and is variable by the use of de-power systems.

### Aspect ratio

A measurement of the shape of a kite. Calculated by dividing the square of the span by the area. This figure is given in two ways: when the kite is laid out flat, or the projected area when it is flying. The first figure is of little use as a high aspect ratio kite often has a low projected (or actual) ratio.

### Asymmetric (board)

A twin-tip board with different shaped rails; only the heel-side rail is usually used as an edge.

### ATB

Abbr. All Terrain Board (mountain boards).

### Axel

A jump with a horizontal rotation around a vertical axis.

### Batten

Stiffener in the kite, usually of fibreglass or carbon fibre; they help to maintain the kite's shape. The same job is also done by inflatable ribs on many kites.

### Bearing away

Steering more downwind.

### Beating

Making a series of tacks, each one taking you slightly upwind, so that when combined with a gybe at each end, you cover the same area of water, or progress upwind.

### Beaufort

Marine scale of wind strengths.

### Big Air

A high jump. A big air competition is one in which the aim is to make as big jumps as possible.

### Bindings (full)

A boot-like system fixed to the board that allows a very secure connection for the rider's feet, usually found on wakeboards. (Sandal) A broad foot strap with an additional heel strap to hold the foot in place, usually found on smaller boards..

### BKSA

British Kitesurfing Association. The UK's governing body.

### Body-dragging

In-water kite control practice without a board.

### Bow kite

An inflatable leading edge design with several bridle connection points on the leading edge, this enables the kites to be supported in a flatter shape than those with connections at the tips alone, and they are therefore more efficient and can be adjusted through a greater de-power range.

### Bridle lines

The lines permanently attached to the kite that help to define its shape.

### Buggies (also parakarts)

3-wheeled land vehicles designed to be powered by traction kites. (Actually 2 and 4-wheel versions are also in use.)

### Carve

Cutting a fast curving line through the water by digging in one edge.

### Carve gybe

Carving a turn at speed where the board remains on the plane.

## Channels

Grooves in the bottom of the board to aid directional stability, usually found on wakeboards.

## Chicken loop

The small loop that activates a de-power system, used by hooking in the harness and allowing the bar to move away, thus transferring load from the rear lines to the front lines and lowering the angle of attack.

## Cumulus (clouds)

Convection clouds, cumulus are usually piled up, rather than flat, and indicate thermal activity and therefore variable winds.

## Custom (board)

A one-off design.

## De-power system

Method of reducing the angle of attack and hence the pull of the kite, using lines attached to the chicken loop of the control bar system.

## Deck

Top of the board.

## Directional

Board with a nose and tail that can only (normally) be ridden nose first.

## Dyneema (also Spectra, Technora)

Trade name for Polyetheylene line material. It is very strong and flexible, making it ideal for kite line.

## Edge

Vb. To dig the rail of the board into the water for directional control.

## Epoxy resin

A common material used in the manufacture of boards.

## Fakie

To ride with the right foot forward. (also Goofy)

## FFVL

Federation Francais de Vol Libre  French Free-Flying Association. This is the governing body of kitesurfing in France. It also governs hang-gliding, paragliding and other traction kite flying.

## Foil

A ram-air kite with cells.

## Freeride

Non-competitive riding.

## Grab

A move where the rider holds the edge of the board during a jump.

## Gybe

Method of changing a kiteboard's direction by turning the nose of the board through the downwind zone.

## Inflatables

Kites requiring pump-up spars and ribs to provide structure and water re-launchability.

## Kite loop

Full 360 rotation of the kite.

## Knot

Measurement of speed, one nautical mile per hour. Equates to 1.15 mph.

## Luff

When the kite becomes totally de-powered because it has travelled beyond the edge of the window. It often dives and flutters down to the water.

## Mountain Board

See ATB.

## Mutant

A twin-tip board with the facility to be reconfigured as a directional.

## No-Foot

A trick where the board is taken off the feet in midair. (Some boards now have a handle for performing this!)

## Off the Lip

A turn made on the crest of a breaker.

## Offshore (Wind)

When the wind blows from the land to the

sea, sometimes known as a 'land breeze'.

## Over powered

When the kite or wind is too much for the rider to handle.

## Paragliding

A form of free flight using a ram-air canopy.

## PKA

Parakart Association; like the BBC, but the PKA concentrates primarily on race meets.

## PKRA

International competition circuit.

## Power band

The sector of the window where the kite is producing significant power.

## Ram-air kite

Double surface kite design relying on movement through the air to maintain its inflated aerodynamic profile.

## Ribs

Inflatable kites: the inflated tubes running fore-aft giving shape to the kite. Ram-air kites: the vertical panels of material separating the individual cells of the kite.

## Rocker

The curvature of the underside of the board. Nose rocker is known as the scoop, tail rocker as the lift.

## Rogallo kites

Single surface kites using rigid tubes for support. Named after the inventor Francis Rogallo.

## Sea breeze

Phenomenon of an onshore wind picking up on warm days.

## Secure position

Top of the window (see Zenith).

## Shore break

The line of surf where the waves break as they approach the beach.

## Skimboards

Small finless boards that have occasionally been powered by kites. They will work in as little as a centimetre of water.

## Snow kiting

Any traction kiting on snow. Skis, sleds and snowboards all work well.

## Stall

When the angle of attack of the aerofoil becomes too high, the airflow breaks away, lift is lost and the kite falls backwards.

## Thermal

Bubble or column of rising air.

## Traction kite

Powerful kite used for pulling a kiteboard, buggy or similar.

## Transition

Switching riding direction (often referred to in jumps, e.g. back loop with transition).

## Toe down

Riding with the toe edge of the board gripping the water; also known as forward-side.

## Twin tips

Boards that can be ridden in either direction without turning.

## Wakeboard

Small type of board used with bindings designed for boat towing and now kitesurfing.

## Wind gradient

Reduction of wind speed near the surface due to friction.

## Window

The available kite positions for a given combination of kite and conditions.

## Windward

Upwind, the direction looking into the wind.

## Zenith

The highest point above the rider's horizon attained by the kite.

# Index